🌿 a life full of surprises

a life full of SURPRISES

LLOYD JOHN OGILVIE

abingdon press / *nashville and new york*

39475

A LIFE FULL OF SURPRISES

Standard Book Number: 687-21847-0

Library of Congress Catalog Card Number: 79-84712

Scripture quotations are from the Revised Standard
Version of the Bible, copyrighted 1946 and 1952 by
the Division of Christian Education, National Council
of Churches, and are used by permission.

SET UP, PRINTED, AND BOUND BY THE
PARTHENON PRESS, AT NASHVILLE,
TENNESSEE, UNITED STATES OF AMERICA

❦ preface

I believe that discouraged churchmen, religious people who have not found a liberating faith, and those who have by-passed the church in a quest for an exciting, adventuresome life, can come alive to the serendipity of life as Christ meant it to be. The purpose of this book is to expose this quality of life as Christ described it in the Sermon on the Mount and as it is being lived by secular saints today. Each dimension of the message from the mount is illustrated with actual stories of people and the experience of a congregation which tried to live it out with faithfulness and obedience in an industrial and academic community, struggling with all the problems and potentials of the last third of the twentieth century. In a time when it is being questioned whether the local, institutional church will survive as a crucial part of God's strategy, this book represents my deep conviction that a congregation can be a viable and flexible center of spiritual experimentation which deploys in the world contagious people who can communicate their faith and participate with Christ in the transformation of society.

The experiences recorded here are part of my lifelong search for authentic Christianity. I long to participate in contemporary expressions of the amazing level of life I see displayed on the pages of the New Testament. The discrepancy between the dull religion found in many churches and the joyous life I sense in the first century church has alarmed me. The endless arguments between personal pietists and social revolutionaries in the church today have troubled me. I have wanted to run with a two-legged gospel. The door which swung open to an exciting life for me was hinged on both life-affirming faith and costly social concern.

I am thankful for the kind of people through whom Christ has invaded my life. Early in my academic career, I was fortunate to meet some people who had the dynamic combination of personal faith and radical involvement in the needs of others. With them I came to know the love and forgiveness of the living Christ and discovered a vision for the renewal of society. Through the years I have tried to celebrate life in honest, open fellowship with others to discern Christ's most daring strategy for me, the church, and our culture. In a covenant group with which I meet consistently, in depth sensitivity relationships with staff teammates and with church officers and members with whom I have been yoked in ministry, I have constantly felt the Master pressing me on to new growth and adventure. I am persistently in search of new ways of sharing the secret of the power of love motivated by the indwelling Christ who enables personal freedom and creative, nonreligious involvement in the world.

My deep appreciation is expressed to Alice Sellers, my secretary and friend, for typing the manuscript through several revisions.

Most of all, I want to dedicate this book to my wife, Mary Jane, and my three children, Heather, Scott, and Andrew, with whom I have found life to be a great happening, a life full of surprises.

New Year's Day, 1969
The Manse, Bethlehem, Pennsylvania

❦ contents

the plan of life as it was meant to be

the purpose of life as it was meant to be

the power of life as it was meant to be

❦ the plan of life as it was meant to be

1 / life as it was meant to be

The most exciting thing I see in our time of history is the new breed of humanity God is raising up out of the traditional church. In the midst of all the bad news about the failure of the church, much of which is more than justified, something now needs to be said about this amazing cadre of people who have come alive and about their churches which are wrestling with what it means to be a liberating fellowship. These are winsome, willing men and women who are constantly surprised by what God is able to do with life completely put under his marching orders. They have a radical freedom expressed in a reconciling ministry. For them there is no tyranny of the either/or. They have both personal faith and social concern— love for Christ and love for the world—time for devotion and time to demonstrate.

The timidity and fear of tradition and religiosity have been exorcised. These are the secular "now" saints who have faced the irreverence of an irrelevant life and are on the move in centers of change and conflict in our world. The problems of living have become the laboratory of growth in joy. A sick and suffering society has become the locale of costly obedience. Corporate structures are being renewed, neighborhoods are being integrated, marriages have been healed, families are discovering a ministry, and initiative love is being communicated to disillusioned people who are hung up or let down in learning how to live.

This authentic Christianity is a quality of life in fellowship with the living Christ who relentlessly challenges men to live life as it was meant to be. He offers men life—life abundant, to the hilt—expectant, enlivened, and empowered. It is life as Christ lived it; life as we live it in him as recipients of his love and forgiveness; and life as he lives it in us as indwelling, enabling power. This is what C. G. Jung declared to be the bold claim of Christianity: that it adds a new rung to the ladder of evolution, producing a new kind of creature who lives in a new way.

The blueprint for this new way of living is the Sermon on the Mount. Here Jesus portrays life as God intends it to be. He gives a plan challenging enough to provide a strategy for living which will make a difference in the world, a purpose adequate to demand all our resources, and a power great enough to liberate a radical love for difficult people in impossible situations in the ambiguities and frustrations of the cybernation and change of our generation, torn with violence and hatred. He shows us who we are, whose we are, and why we are in the world. We are to be amazed as we discover this life in the very things which defeat and debilitate other men. It is to be lived out in costly involvement in the gray grimness of man's confusion.

When Jesus saw the crowds which flocked to him, he discerned their basic need was to live—really live. He saw their anxiety over daily life, their inability to love deeply, their lack of adventure and hope for the future, and their joyless countenances. It was because of their need that this one who said, "I have come that you might have life," went up onto the mount and, as the "one greater than Moses," called his disciples to him to share with them the essential meaning of life which would both fulfill and supersede the ancient law. He gave them the portrait of life so that they could share it with the world.

The same is true today. Christ is calling his church to rediscover and live the abundant life in depth. Again, he sees the need of the multitude, and the church is to be the channel of communication. The same needs for life which Jesus saw then are magnified and multiplied in our tumultuous, revolutionary times. Beneath the movements which capture people's loyalty today and demand their allegiance is the lust for life. Hippie and yippie, social revolutionary, black militant, political agitator, and student demonstrator—all want to find life. They are angered and frustrated by the forces which have debilitated people. The sickness of our culture is being exposed and attacked. We may not like the form of the reaction, but we must see the underlying quest for meaning and purpose. At the same time, we must be free to confess the inadequacy of our own false gods of our making and faking.

This can be the finest, most exciting hour in the history of the church. The greatest gift we have to offer the world is an incarnation of life as it was meant to be lived. As revolutionary reconcilers we are to outlive and forgive, outcare and dare the world!

But can this happen to the church as we know it? Can the bound Gullivers in the contemporary church tied tightly by the twines of the past, personal problems, fears and frustrations, the rites and rules of religion, be cut loose to become free men? I believe they can. What happens to people who take Christ seriously, who dare to live his manifesto of life in the Sermon on

11

the Mount and become renewing agents in the world, is the compelling good news I want to share. How these people got started, how they grew—how their churches were renewed, what they are doing to change society—is the new chapter in the book of Acts being lived in our time.

2 / rooted in grace

I heard a man in our church described recently, "He's so alive! What a stodgy, boring person he used to be! I am amazed at the difference! He seems so vital, so involved with people, so warm and loving. But most of all, he's expectant—as if at any moment something new and exciting is going to happen. And you know—it usually does!"

But what must we do to discover a life like that? Where do we begin? We must start where Jesus begins the Beatitudes: with an experience of grace which manifests itself in joy.

Joy is the key word which best describes this style of life. It is the essence of the idea Jesus used to introduce each of the aspects of the quality of life he came to make possible. The identifiable outward characteristic of a Christian is joy. The Greek word for blessed, *makarios,* comes close to our word for happy, but goes much deeper. Happiness is dependent on the circumstances and surroundings in which we find ourselves. The root of the word is "hap," which means chance. We are happy if things are going well, and we are agreeable. Joy is way beyond this transitory condition. As a matter of fact, it is discovered in the change, conflict, disturbance, loss, and confusion which often make others unhappy. Joy is unassailable, untouchable, undisturbable. Each of the Beatitudes presents a paradox. Yet when we understand the deeper meaning of the seemingly contradictory truths in each, we learn that Jesus is showing us that true joy is to be experienced in the very things most men abhor because they do not understand.

Joy is the outward manifestation of the inner experience of grace. Life as it was meant to be is rooted in grace. That's where it all begins. Grace is God's unmerited, unchanging, unmotivated, uncalculated love for us just as we are. Life really begins for us when we are healed in the depth of our nature by a love like that, and face each situation fortified by the courage it enables. Grace is God's essential attitude toward us. It is his love in action in us, through us, and around us. Out of grace he created us; as grace incarnate he lived among us as the Christ and suffered the cross that we might have a tangible sign of the limitless extent of his love; and in grace he persistently invades our lives to show us the inadequacy of our self-justifying efforts. There is nothing we can do or be to earn this grace. But there is a realization which makes it possible to receive it.

That's just what Jesus meant in the first two Beatitudes. Poverty of spirit and mourning are essential ingredients of a crisis which makes possible the experience of grace which results in joy. A crisis is that point in a sickness which indicates whether the result is to be recovery or death. It is the turning point—a crucial, decisive time. A crisis is perhaps one of the most important gifts life has to offer. It is in a crisis that our sense of need is discovered. We are faced with reality and forced to see life as it is. The most serious sickness is the sickness of not knowing we are sick; there is no greater need than that of not knowing we are in need. Jesus knew this; that's why he began with the necessity of a crisis. The first Beatitude deals with the crisis of personal need and the second with the focus of this crisis in the interpersonal and social.

The Greek word used to translate Jesus' word for "poor" is a very severe word. It is *ptōchos,* which means absolutely and completely poor. This kind of poverty of the spirit means that some frustration, fear, or failure has pressed us to realize that we are at the end of our resources, ingenuity, and clever answers. We are forced to recognize that we can change neither ourselves nor our circumstances without help. Our self-improvement programs are but a rearrangement of the status quo. Life has brought us to the end of our rope; time is running out; there is no hope in ourselves. There is nothing to do but cry out, "O God, if there is a god—help me!" That's the core of the experience that opens us to receive grace—and express joy.

"But must I go through a crisis to admit my need?" a man asked me recently. I have come to the point in my thinking and experience where I must answer "Yes!" Most of the people I know who are living vital Christian lives began and have grown in crises which exposed their emptiness and insufficiency. But we do not need to go hunting for a crisis. We need to recognize the ones we are in already.

This is what Jesus means by mourning. It's more than grief over the death of a loved one, though that may be its temporary focus. We experience true mourning when we allow our hearts to be broken by the things which break the heart of God. This happens when we dare to look across the yawning cavern between what is and what could be—in ourselves, in others, and in society.

This same man who asked the question above was later faced with a crisis he could not handle. The crisis was mounting when he asked the question, but he did not know it. The bottom fell out of his life when his son rejected his values, morals, and way of life. His busy life had brought him professional recognition, but he had never taken time to communicate with his son. The doctor in the New York hospital for dope addiction where the boy was admitted for treatment put it to him directly: "The trouble with your son is that he doesn't know what it means to be a man. Either you didn't know yourself, or you never took time to give your son a pattern of what living is all about."

We mourn when we see what we have done with the gift of life and realize how quickly it is slipping away. Mourning is seeing what we have done to the people in our lives. It's sensing the need in other people for acceptance and love and admitting our judgments and self-centeredness. Or it's when we feel love but are too bound up to express it in costly ways. We mourn when we long for a breakthrough to deep communication but feel the tension of a relationship filled with anger and hurt.

This is the kind of mourning experienced by a couple who were called in by the psychiatrist of their daughter's school. They were told that she was failing because of tensions which were traceable to their home. He talked about the girl and asked some penetrating questions about the parents' relationship to each other. From this point he moved more deeply into their individual childhoods.

After subsequent visits the couple became honest about their life. They faced attitudes which were crippling their family life. They realized that they had never talked about what they really needed and wanted out of life. They both confessed their need for love and their inability to accept each other's language and way of love. It was a painful year as the real crisis crystallized. Both husband and wife were crushed when they realized their

16

unwillingness to grow up even though they both were in their late thirties.

The break in the deadlock came when the husband experienced the power of God's liberating grace. He had been a part of a church all his life, but it took the crisis of lovelessness to open his mind and heart to what he had heard all his life. Another member of the laity, who had gone through a similar problem and was willing to open his inner life for the man to see, helped him to begin with the immediate problem and then went deeper to help him in a complete trust of his whole life to Christ, asking for the gift of love and the freedom to love those around him naturally and creatively.

It wasn't long before his wife found the same power to love through Christ. For both, the change came at the desperate end of their own ability to find an answer.

We mourn in these crises of spiritual inadequacy. Life offers the gift of people who need answers which we do not have, or long for meaning and purpose which we are unable to communicate. We are thrust into the problems of our friends and associates whom we can do little to help. Nothing can happen through us until it has happened to us. We cannot give something away that we do not have. In these days of new emphasis on social action among Christians many people are discovering that they have little to offer others when they do get involved. Confronted with the complex problems in society, they realize the inadequacy of their altruism to sustain them in conflict and resistance.

According to Christ mourning is to see that the sickness of society is but the need of our own hearts written large. We mourn when we allow race and poverty problems to get to us where we feel; when we internalize the anguish of an unwed

17

mother or the rebellion of a teen-age dropout. Often it is through involvement in these tension-oriented situations that we realize what the disciples must have realized when they could not heal the man's son at the foot of the Mount of Transfiguration. After Jesus had healed him, they asked the painful question prompted by the crisis of realizing their impotency, "Why couldn't we do that?" Well, why couldn't they?

But there are also the crises of opportunity. At a time we expect it least, a challenge comes to us, and we must decide what to do. The alternative possibilities are attractive; the danger of a mistake is grave. I am reminded of many people who have started to pray honestly and earnestly when they recognized their need to know what they should do. These gentle but demanding questions often help: "What do you think God wants you to do? Have you asked him?" It's amazing how many traditional church members have never reevaluated the basic direction of their lives. They want God's help to live out lives which have never been checked by his reorienting guidance. I think of a man who is now a powerful Christian, but who first got started in the new life when he went through financial problems and had to realize his false values and distorted securities in the kingdom of thingdom. For another man it was a professional problem. He was bypassed at work in a reshuffle of key executives. This led to a reappraisal of goals. For the first time he realized that he had never asked God to guide his future. Work had been *his* business; he would see God in church. Now, through the crisis, he has discovered the power of God to guide all his decisions.

It's not easy to admit our need. We have insulated ourselves with material prosperity, overwork, positions of power, the right friends. We all have our favorite kind of anesthesia to deaden the realization of reality. Religious activity is used by many of us.

18

We can become so involved in church that we never have to question the direction of our lives. I remember how shocked some people were when we wrote a confession of our crises of emptiness in the corporate prayer of confession for the Sunday worship. This language was so direct and contemporary no one could miss it. It broke into the safety of the church which for some was merely an escape from reality. Worship became a crisis of exposure rather than beautiful presentation to be observed.

Thank God for crises! In them we sense our need. When things fall apart or life around us demands what we do not have, then we can honestly admit our need. And then the same gracious God who was with us in the crises will meet us at the point of our need.

The Philippian jailer's question to Paul is where we begin: "What must I do to be saved?"

"Nothing! You already are!" is God's gracious reply to those whose need has driven them to him. In this context Paul could answer the jailer: "Accept the love God has offered in Jesus Christ, which you can never earn or deserve. You belong to him. That will never change. He loves you, forgives you, accepts you. Believe that, and you will know for yourself what is already true!"

That's grace. The experience cancels out our basic motives of self-justification and reorients our whole life around the liberating secret of God's initiative love. God has loved us all through our self-defeating efforts at independence. He has waited patiently for us to realize the love that was there all along. We respond to God, not in order to receive his love, but because we already have received his love. We ask for forgiveness, a way out of a complex situation, a power to love, and a direction for the future because God is ready to give long before we are ready to receive.

This kind of love will never change; he loves us as much right now as he ever will—more than we can imagine. We do not need to be good enough, faithful enough, or obedient enough to deserve it. These things will come naturally, not as prerequisites but as the result.

This is the creative confidence of joyous living. We have been called out of love to be God's people, to be filled with his Spirit, to communicate his love. We need nothing or no one; therefore we can use everything and serve everyone to glorify God and enjoy him. Now our only question is how to live out this depth security in every area of life.

This is the quality of life I see among traditional Christians who are coming alive. Because a sense of need has opened them up to God's love, they are now recipients of the tremendous promise which Jesus gave in these first Beatitudes. The kingdom of God is theirs, and they are comforted. The two go together. The kingdom is God's rule, and comfort is the assurance of the Comforter, another name of the present power of the living God. The grace we have received enables us to desire God's will in all things. When we get out on a limb in faithful obedience, he is there with us; when we are weak, he is our strength; when we are uncertain, he is our source of fresh guidance; when we are discouraged, he is our courage.

The people who have experienced this are joining Paul as "the people who have turned the world upside down." Their neat little worlds have been turned upside down by a profound experience and then right side up by the reorienting ministry of the Spirit. There is an inseparable relationship between grace and guidance, faith and obedience, freedom and responsibility. We cannot change the world by our own strength or clever programs. The world will be changed by people who have been changed by the power of God's love. This alone can impute the toughness and tenderness needed by the people who would move through God's agenda which is written in the needs of people and the horrendous suffering in our society. The authentic quality of life needed to meet these needs must be rooted in grace but then expressed in abandonment. It is to this expression that we must now press on.

3 / expressed in abandonment

Some time ago, a full-page ad appeared in the *Wall Street Journal* with an interest-arresting title. In bold black letters across the top of the page were words which would be irresistible to a person at any age—"How To Retire At 35."

I read the advertisement immediately. Though I had passed thirty-five, I wanted to know what I had missed. This is what it said:

It's so easy. Thousands of men do it every year. In all walks of life. And it sets our economy, our country, and the world back thousands of years in terms of wasted human resources. But worst of all, it is the personal tragedy that almost always results from "early retirement."

It usually begins with a tinge of boredom. Gradually a man's work begins to seem endlessly repetitious. The rat race hardly seems worth it any more.

It is at this point that many a 35 year old boy wonder retires. There are no testimonial dinners or gold watches. He goes to work every day, puts in his forty hours, and even draws a pay check. He's retired, but nobody knows it. Not at first, anyhow.

The lucky ones get fired in time to make a fresh start. Those less fortunate hang on for a while—even decades—waiting and wondering; waiting for a raise or promotion that never comes, and wondering why. With the life expectancy approaching the century mark, 65 years is a long time to spend in a rocking chair.[1]

I put down the paper, but the challenging, prophetic words kept disturbing me. I began to think of the many people I knew like that. Before my mind's eye marched the countless numbers who have retired intellectually and spiritually. The startling realization was that most of these people were still climbing the ladder of success professionally and would look at retirement as absurd. Yet, they have retired from life.

The traditional church is filled with retired Christians and dropout disciples. These are the religious people who know little of God, seldom have a viable experience of faith, and are uninvolved in the crises swirling about them in the world. They checked their idealisms long ago. Change is disturbing, and controversial issues are avoided. Convictions, values, and dreams are blighted by the pressures to conform; the lust for security has become a virulent virus in their bloodstream; and the need for things has won their allegiance. The cherished hopes of a vital life have been engulfed in the endless tide of living, raising a family, and keeping the bills paid. The Christian faith is an addendum to an already complete life. The contradiction between what they believe and what's going on in the world doesn't hurt any more. They have retired.

These are the gray Christians. They are neutral, agnostic. God may be at work in the world, others may experience his life-changing love, but somehow this does not happen to them. All too often the church is part of their retirement program. It pays handsome benefits of comfort, reassurance, and activity which give the illusion of involvement. Church work is substituted for the real work of the church. And as an institution, debilitated

[1] Prepared by Marsteller Inc. and used with their permission.

23

by the reservations of these people in positions of leadership, the church becomes a bastion of defense against change and renewal in our society.

Jesus discerned this same rigidity in the people who came to him longing for life. I believe this was the reason he went on in the Beatitudes to dramatize life. Having made clear how the new life is begun with an experience of grace, he went on to show that this grace enables freedom. He used a word which is strange to our ears and raises up distorted ideas because of its confused contemporary implications—*meek*.

The word translated as meekness does not mean convictionless, spineless weakness. It really means moldability. The Greek word used for meekness is *praus,* one use of which describes a wild animal which has been tamed and brought under control, able to respond to a master's reins. What an image that conjures up for us! Only a completely God-controlled man can find perfect freedom. George Matheson was right in praying, "Make me a captive, Lord, and then I shall be free." Jesus' meek men are free to be molded in his image. A deep, penetrating experience of God's grace issues forth in a "creative carelessness" which is the essence of vital Christian character. The one word which sums up what Jesus was getting at as a part of the characteristics of joyous living is *abandonment.* Meekness is abandonment.

There are many tired, worn phrases which are used to express the nature of man's response to grace. We hear about commitment, dedication, surrender, and consecration. All these words contain an aspect of what our response should be. But they are all overused and suggest too much self-justifying effort to meet God's demands, prompting human judgment and exclusiveness. I like the word *abandonment* because it forces us to realize that any response to God's grace in Christ is inadequate unless it

24

brings us to a total relinquishment of ourselves and our control over our life. Abandonment involves letting go of the past and morbid self-incrimination over our failures. It means that we see our present life in our jobs, families, possessions, as the clay for the Potter of Life to mold in his own way. It is the willingness to allow God to penetrate into our personalities to show us our true selves. There can be no hidden reserve, no unexplored thought. The sin against the Holy Spirit which Jesus talked about is to say "No" to God. The abandoned man says "Yes." Thus, the future is alive with unlimited possibilities. Abandonment enables us to dare, innovate, fail, change, begin anew every day. The old expressions of conformity, such as, "We never did it that way before," are replaced by a faithfulness and obedience which prays, "Lord, show me what you want me to do, show me with whom I am to do it, and give me courage to do it."

When I think of abandonment as our response to God's gracious love, a very different kind of unretired Christian marches before my mind's eye. What I want to say about these people is illustrated in the true story of a man I will call Sam.

It was about four in the morning when Sam was awakened by an uneasy disquiet within him. The events of the past weeks had left him alarmed and disturbed. Though he longed for sleep to return, he could not keep from ruminating over what seemed to be happening to his life. He realized that the thing he most feared might happen to him was just what was happening. His life had become irrelevant, and he knew it. What difference did it make that he was living in his generation? He thought of the world condition. It produced an overall feeling of frustration—war, poverty, riots, racial tension, industrial strife, student unrest, lawlessness—revolts because of revolting conditions.

"And what can I do about it?" he thought.

This question focused in on an even more profound question: "Do I have an answer to the riddle of life which, if applied, could be the solution to these problems in the world?"

But then he got defensive. "How can I solve these problems if I can't work out my own?" he reflected. He thought of some of the tensions he felt growing in his marriage and family. The spark had gone out somehow. Neither Sam nor his wife had ever been unfaithful or cruel, but the romance was all over, it seemed. They went through the motions, but both had a feeling that marriage had a lot more to offer than they were finding. Just the evening before, his wife had said, "Sam, what's wrong with us? You have looked so old and drawn lately. You seem impatient with me and the kids. I feel lonely and cut off from you. I've tried to reach you, but you are so preoccupied with all you are doing. I am beginning not to care, and that frightens me."

He had put her off with a glib reassurance, but now her words haunted him. His times with the kids were filled with correction and fussy admonitions. They didn't seem to appreciate how good he was to them, and the teen-agers were beginning to suggest that their life was rather phony.

Sam thought about work, but that only added to his feeling of frustration. The day had not gone well there either. Nothing had seemed to work out as he had planned it. Several clients called to complain about deliveries and the quality of some recent production. His boss was on him about things, and his "name on the door rates a Bigelow on the floor" security didn't give him the satisfaction that it had so often before when things didn't go just his way.

"Who are you anyway, Sam?" he thought.

"You are like a rubber band being stretched in a thousand

directions. Family, office, civic groups, church, friends—they all think they own you. Pay the bills, do your job, don't offend anyone, make everyone like you—keep things smooth, Sam, and you will be all right."

In his restlessness he had a fleeting thought about Christ. That made him think of his church and his responsibilities as a church school teacher and officer. That just made him feel more guilty and raised up all sorts of "ought" feelings inside. Church was just more responsibilities, not a lot different from all the committees in the community on which he served. He wondered how Jesus would make out in the asphalt jungle of a technopolis with cybernation and computers.

Sam remembered a group of men from his church who met for lunch each week near his office to talk about what it means to be a Christian in the complexities and ambiguities of today's world. He had carefully avoided this and dozens of other small groups for spontaneous discussion, sharing of concerns, and prayer, which were meeting all over the community under the sponsorship of his church. Now, for some reason, perhaps because of the power he observed in the lives of some of the people in those groups, he determined to look in on the group for businessmen the next day.

At the meeting he found out that he was not the only one troubled with the danger of irrelevancy. That day the group was grappling with a portion of the Sermon on the Mount which had been exposited in the sermon the Sunday before. They were zeroing in on the Beatitude, "Blessed are the meek, for they shall inherit the earth."

The word *meek* immediately brought Uriah Heep and Casper Milquetoast to Sam's mind. Inherit the earth? Not in his world!

You have to be firm, aggressive, and decisive. What did this Beatitude mean for contemporary Christians?

The discussion leader for that day gave a brief introduction. He interpreted the Beatitude with the assistance of a study guide prepared to help discussion in the context of the previous Sunday's sermon. He suggested that an aspect of the meaning of meekness was abandonment—a combination of openness, willingness, and freedom to discover God's will and do it. He went on to say that the meek man was one who was so overjoyed with God's graciousness that he has a freedom to be himself, accept and love himself, and have love for other people. That caught Sam's attention; the Christian faith had never meant that to him.

The men began to talk honestly about how they had found Christ's power to be real only after they had turned the reins of their lives over to his management. They talked openly about personal needs, their families, pressures on the job, and then began to talk about some of the troubled places in the community. What did meekness mean for all of that? The conclusion seemed to be that there was power available to them for these needs if they would be open to guidance, ready to receive, and completely open to be used by Christ. This was not "church talk" as Sam had experienced it in endless committee meetings at church, but down to earth, practical, and applicable to real life as these men knew it. This was authentic. There were no clichés or stuffy religiosity. Everything Sam had been through in the past few days—years, for that matter—prepared him to listen, and then participate intently.

The discussion hit a high point of intensity around a final question: "If you loved Christ with all your heart, and were willing to do anything he wanted you to do, what would you like most to do with your life? If Christ can guide our lives, why not trust him that the very thing we would like most to do as an expression of abandonment and love has been motivated by him? What needs healing and reconciliation? Why not get involved and do it with all you've got?"

The group closed with the most unstudied, honest prayers Sam had ever heard. These men were not saying prayers; they were really talking to God. Each talked simply about his own need for spiritual power, relationships which needed liberating love, and particular problems in the community in which God could guide them to become involved.

Sam realized his spiritual bankruptcy. For all his goodness and religious activity, he had to admit that he had never turned the management of his life over to the lordship of Christ—past, present, and future—mind and emotions—job, plans, and purposes—family, finances, property. It was the sense of freedom in these men which hooked him. What about his life?

In his halting prayer Sam took up the challenge to begin where he was spiritually with what he had, and give what he knew of himself in both problems and possibilities to however much he knew of Christ at that moment. And then he asked for specific marching orders for a relevant ministry in some areas of injustice where his life could count. It was a real response for Sam and, in a way, a reporting back for duty after being A.W.O.L. from responsibility.

The answers to these and other prayers came powerfully in the following months. He met consistently with the group. Each week the men took a personal involvement inventory. They checked their goals, resources, and strategy and tried to enable one another to discover and invest the particular gifts for ministry given to each man.

Sam became more sensitive to the need around him than ever

before. Suddenly he was aware. No longer did he look for meaning in his work; he brought meaning to his work. He became involved in the lives of the people with whom he worked. He learned to listen for the subtle pleas for help and began to feel the anxiety and tension around him. His prayers for people opened him up to them and equipped him with a deep empathetical love for those whom he had overlooked or relegated to categories of his severe judgments. As he earned the right through deep relationships of costly caring, he was able to share with others what had happened to him.

Soon he became concerned about his "segregated heart" which had resisted integration in his suburb. Previously he had signed a petition to keep a black family from moving into a home on his beautiful street lined with lovely homes. The neighbors had always said that if a cultured, educated, economically capable black ever wanted to live in their section, there would be no problem. But something always went amiss. Now Sam became active to see that nothing would go wrong and helped get a home near him sold to a black. The hostility of neighbors, the rejection expressed by his friends, and the danger to his professional advancement were all faced with a new sense of the power of love.

Sam had prayed for a relevant life and his prayers were being answered. His family was transformed as he and his wife found new romance and fun together. This affection spilled over to the children. They joined him in concern for people, and their home became a place where troubled people knew they were welcome at any hour. The family discovered a mutual ministry which drew them together.

The last time I saw Sam, his face was alive with joy. There

was new vitality in his body, and his voice had a ring of new conviction and courage.

What happened to this man and countless others like him should be everyday Christianity for all of us. I have told his story here at length because he and others in his church exemplify the people who are inheriting the earth. Because they have lost control of their lives to Christ, they have new self-control, new power for life's demands, new direction for their decisions, and new hope for the future. They now know that Paul was right—"all things are yours." Their only question now is, "Where do we go from here?" That necessitates a strategy.

4 / guided by a strategy

"Young man, stick to the gospel! Your job is to tell us about God's love, not to disturb us. I come to church to find spiritual strength, not to be upset. The church ought to be one place I can find peace, but instead I feel uneasy and disquieted. It isn't the way it used to be. Keep off these controversial issues; stop trying to change our personal lives; give us some assurance."

The respected church member of long years of faithful service spoke intently across the luncheon table. He meant his words to be kind counsel and challenge, but his tone indicated that he was personally hurt and unsettled by what was happening to him and his church. It was a moment of truth and honesty between friends. He had spoken his mind; now it was my turn.

"Wonderful!" I said. "Sounds like Christ is at work in your life."

Then I went on to tell him that to be a Christian meant to be disturbed by a divine discontent. The authentic test that shows we have abandoned our lives to the management of Christ is that we have deep dissatisfaction with our personal growth, are unsettled by unhealed relationships, and are indignant toward injustice in any area of our culture. We were meant for a ministry of mercy in which we share the love we have received wherever people suffer. Christ will never allow us to stagnate at any stage of growth. He abhors the status quo as nature abhors a vacuum.

This man had become a Christian years before in a very moving experience of God's love. He had tried to read his Bible faithfully through the years and was a trusted officer of the church. Yet he had never been able to talk about his faith in a personal way. Though he was concerned about several people in his life, he was able to give them little more than superficial, pious advice and moralisms. His convictions about social problems were based on his political and economic preconceptions and had seldom been examined in the light of the gospel he wanted me to "stick to."

As we talked further during this and subsequent luncheons, we went deeply into our strategies for living. We talked about Christ and marriage, our kids, professional hopes and ambitions, hidden fears and unforgiven memories. I asked him, "Being as honest as you can, what are the basic things which drive and shape your life?" As I opened myself to him and let him see me as I was, we both discovered anew that you cannot stand still. He began to tell about areas of his life which he had never shared with anyone. We talked about life's basic relationships which Jesus focused—with God, ourselves, others, and the world. Then we began to think about God's strategy for each of these areas. Soon he was off dead-center and on the move, perhaps for the first time since he had gotten started spiritually years before. He took a new look at his home, his church, his job, and Christ's plan for him in the future. This man is still disturbed, but now it's a different kind of disturbance—a creative disturbance initiated by the living Christ, bringing about not resistance but renewal. His concern now is not to keep things as they are, but to

33

change them, beginning with himself, to what they were meant to be.

What's disturbing you? What kind of things trouble you? What fires your indignation? What is it in yourself, your family, your friends, your world, that makes you dissatisfied?

When we are honest about what makes us discontent, we can discern what drives us. Our indignations show us the imperatives by which we live. This inventory shows us quickly whether we are dealing with soul-sized issues or are piddling in the polluted eddies of irrelevant self-pity.

I am convinced that the reason most people do not find life exciting is that they have never discovered a strategy which is daring and demanding enough to stretch their minds, marshal their energies, and challenge their resourcefulness. We all crave adventure; we all need to be significant; and we all want to feel that our lives are crucial for someone or something. The reason some of us retreat from responsibility, while others of us lose ourselves in a frantic search for meaning in a multiplicity of activities, a sloth of overinvolvement, is simply that we need a galvanizing reason for living which can give our lives a strategy.

In the fourth and fifth Beatitudes, Jesus gives us the formula for discovering a strategy for life: Desire multiplied by righteousness equals mercy in life's relationships. "Joyous are those who desire to be right with God in all relationships of life by sharing the merciful love they have received."

The words Jesus used for desire—hunger and thirst—are not gentle words. They are drastic words which denote hunger to the point of starvation and thirst to the point of dehydration. We find it difficult to understand what he meant. Few who read this book have ever seriously questioned the source of the next meal, much less been dangerously in need of nutrition. Most of us can turn on a tap and get water at the temperature and in the quantity we desire at the moment. Even the occasional water shortages we have had in recent years have never forced us to think any more seriously than how often we should wash either one of the status symbols we park in our garages. Hunger and thirst? We don't know what the words mean.

Perhaps the only way we can get inside of what Jesus seeks to communicate to us is to shift the metaphorical image. For example, remember some time when your body longed, yearned, for rest after an excruciating ordeal; or reflect on the intense, urgent desire to bring someone back to life who has been snatched away in the clutches of death. Remember how you felt? Or perhaps you can recapture the feeling of concern you have had for a loved one—child, friend, lover. You want to help, but you can't! Or do you remember a desire for someone or something more than life itself? When have you really wanted, needed, desired with exigency, urgency, and avidity? What do you want or need that much? Health, love, freedom? The kind of desire Jesus is talking about is the kind on which life depends; without which we cannot go on.

Those who desire righteousness this much are the blessed— the truly joyous. The quality of joy which Jesus exemplified, which he promised his disciples, and which could not be destroyed by change of circumstances or conditions, is discoverable only by those who have experienced a dominant desire for righteousness and have been deeply disturbed by their lack of it.

But what is this righteousness? Put simply, it is rightness with God. A man is righteous who is in a right relationship with God, and the joyous man, according to Jesus, is one who desires this more than all else. How does this occur?

Consider it this way. God created us for fellowship with him-

35

self. But he also created us as free agents with the awesome capacity of free will to choose. We know the dreadful record of man's misuse of this freedom and his desire to run his own life. Sin is this rebellion and mutiny against God. We all know it and express it. In Jesus Christ, God invaded this bastille of self-generated independence and revealed that he loved and forgave man in spite of what he was and had done. The cross was a cosmic atonement, to make "at-one" again the relationship for which man was created. Those who believe in Christ and accept the love offered through him become righteous as a gift.

But the grammar of the Greek in this Beatitude challenges us. Usually, when the verbs of hunger and thirst are used, the partitive genitive case is the rule following the verb. A portion of the thing hungered or thirsted for is what is desired, not the whole. But in the Beatitude righteousness takes the direct accusative, indicating that it is the whole thing which is desired. This means the whole of righteousness, which affects not only our relationship with God or a portion of our life, but all of life. The righteous relationship with God is to pervade all relationships and all responsibilities in every realm of our existence. God has something to say about all of life and how it shall be lived. That spells out the shape of a strategy.

Righteousness implies mercy. I believe that this is why Jesus coupled these two so closely in the Beatitudes. They are part of one experience. Anyone who has experienced God's righteousness through forgiving mercy becomes mercy incarnated to others. What he has received he now must give. As he empties himself in merciful caring for others, he is able to receive more mercy from God.

The full force of the word *mercy* is very challenging. The Hebrew word for mercy, *hesedh,* is a very difficult word to translate. It is quite literally to get inside a person and experience what he is experiencing, feel what he is feeling, know what he knows. This is more than sympathy or even empathy. It is a deliberate identification with a person: to hear with his ears, see with his eyes, sense with his emotions.

This kind of mercy takes time. We cannot really know another person without long periods together. If we are to get inside other people we need to observe them under different circumstances and situations. We must sharpen our insight and discernment. Then we must listen. People usually say two things: what the words sound and what the person means. We get inside another person's mind by careful listening to tone as well as word. With love we let our feelings go in a deep involvement in what the other person is going through. How would I feel if I lived in these same circumstances? How did I feel in similar ones? A merciful person has lived deeply and fully. The result is that he has a point of reference for experiencing vicariously the things another person is facing.

What Jean-Paul Sartre said about sin in another context is also true for us. It can be the "systematic substitution of the abstract for the concrete." That's just our problem when we talk about mercy. We hide in abstractions. We can talk about general needs and problems without concretizing the specific relationships of life where this quality of giving and forgiving love is desperately needed.

Let's start with ourselves. A strategy for living begins there. Are we more severe with ourselves than God would be? Are we still filled with memories of past failures and expect little more for the future? An essential prerequisite to loving others is a healthy love for ourselves as loved by God. I can vividly remember when this became real to me. When I realized that my attempts at humility and selflessness were inverted pride and accepted myself, the gifts God gave me, and the opportunities open to me, I was liberated from self-concern to a new love toward others. My only concern now is all the energy I wasted on needless self-justification.

What about the people in our lives? What is God's strategy there? It's tragic how we withhold mercy from others until they reach our standards or do what we want them to do. We engineer the people around us with our guilt-producing judgments expressed in words and attitudes. We get people on edge so that we can control them through our superior criticisms. What if God had waited until we were adequate? Is there anyone in our life to whom we have not expressed as much mercy as we have received? Anything separating us from any other person? What did we do to cause it? Have we offered unmerited forgiveness to open the way for reconciliation? Anyone come to mind? That's the next step of strategy for us.

I think of a young woman who was filled with hate for her husband, who had been unfaithful. It wasn't until she faced her own failures in less obvious ways and received God's forgiveness that, as an expression of praise to God, she began to love her husband with all of his inconsistencies. He was amazed at the change in her. Eventually he found the source of her love in God's mercy and faced himself as he was, and experienced a profound change in his life.

What about the strategy for society? Christopher Fry's judge was right: "The church has made an honest lady out of the Almighty and it is afraid to let her out in the street again." But out in the streets he goes. Dare we follow? Where is mercy most needed today? In your community or mine?

A steel executive who had a profound experience of mercy in

his personal life began to study the need for righteousness in our community. He found that an astounding number of boys were ready to be paroled but could not be because of the lack of a sponsor. He adopted a Puerto Rican lad who was in serious trouble with the police, was estranged from his disrupted family, had failed in school, and was a member of a hard street gang. There was little hope in life for him when this man from our congregation opened his heart, time schedule, pocketbook, and home to him. It has not been easy to care for him. It has taken hours, patience, and endurance. One night he spent most of the night going from bar to bar searching for him. He has appeared in court when the lad needed a friend. But the results have been gratifying. Through his relationships with this man and spiritually contagious young people, this boy has experienced Christ's mercy, and is on the way in becoming a Christian. But it's not a simple thing for him. A short time ago he was beaten up by his old street gang because of his faith. He did not fight back. He tried to love as he had been loved. He has been able to get a group of younger boys together to share his new faith. He is constantly surprised by what Christ can do with his life now, and the future is exciting.

The important thing about this story is not only what happened to this one lad but what that executive is doing to extend this ministry to others. A community program is being developed in cooperation with the courts, and many other men are being involved. God gave a strategy for a larger need through one man whose joy in righteousness spilled over in mercy.

What is the result of all this? Joyous satisfaction. We will be filled to satisfaction—the satisfaction of knowing that we are part of God's strategy. We will know life's greatest ebullient quality if we desire righteousness more than anything else and, having experienced it, express mercy to others.

The advice of the senior church officer was right. He didn't know what he was saying when he charged, "Stick to the gospel!" We are both learning more all the time of what that means. The gospel really spells out God's strategy. It's the good news of righteousness and mercy. If we stick to that, we will continue to experience joyous, disturbing times.

5 / full of surprises

             In a community where I lived
for a time there was a store which delighted children from eight
to eighty. There was no limit to the unusual things which this
store offered. It was fun to shop there because, no matter what
you went in to buy, you would be amazed at what was available.
The store was called "The Surprise Shop." I believe God means
life to be like that store—full of surprises, never dull, and always
amazing.

We often hear the saying, "Life is full of surprises!" when
some unanticipated challenge, solution, or turn of events occurs.
That is because God is full of surprises. His resourcefulness is
limitless. His interventions are often unexpected, and his answers
are never altogether what we thought. Life in fellowship with
him is vital because, beyond all that we can plan, anticipate, or
hope, he has resources with which to surprise us, which in our
wildest expectations we could never have calculated.

C. S. Lewis, the late English author, entitled his autobiography
with words which capture the adventure of the Christian life.
He described his encounter with God as *Surprised by Joy.* That's
what being a Christian ought to mean. Whenever things seem
impossible, whenever we have painted ourselves into a corner by
our foolish mistakes, and whenever our backs are against the

wall of human inadequacy, watch carefully, listen intently, wait patiently—God is about to enter the drama with something or someone that will knock us back on our heels exclaiming, "Now why didn't I think of that?" The Christian life is life surprised by God. Once we have become involved with Christ as a part of his strategy for our time of history, we begin to experience a serendipitous quality of life. We make extraordinary discoveries in the ordinary circumstances of life. Life becomes a "happening" and each new challenge, opportunity, or problem becomes the occasion for the discovery of some new aspect of his limitless, providential power.

This is the promise Jesus makes in the sixth Beatitude, based on an essential prerequisite: the pure in heart will see God. There is an inescapable interrelationship between what is in our hearts and the surprising things we will be able to see of God at work in our victories and disappointments. But that's just the problem. Jesus tells us that in the heart of man, at the headspring of the rivers of his activity, the waters are polluted. We cannot see God because our hearts are not pure. What does this mean?

The word *heart* needs some clarification. Jesus used it to describe the inner dimensions of personality. It is inclusive of mind, emotions, and will and therefore the source of motives, values, and images which shape our life. It is inward and secret, known by each person alone. Jesus placed tremendous emphasis on the condition of the inner heart. For him, this, not conditions in our lives, was the source of our problems. "There is nothing outside a man which by going into him can defile him . . . for from within, out of the heart of a man, come evil thoughts." (Read Mark 7:15, 21.)

He then goes on to list frustrations of life which come as direct projections of the heart. As a man thinks, so is he in his

42

feelings and his choices. A man's life—associations, responsibilities, involvements, expenditures—will never be different until the heart is different.

Look at it this way: what happens to us or what we cause to happen becomes a problem because of what's inside us. Problems are the focus of our inner condition on the normal and abnormal perplexities of living. The ambience of our environment is the result of the attitudes of our inner selves. Whether our difficulties have been caused by forces in nature, the failures of others, or our own foolishness, they become problems because of us. We react to situations and blame others, circumstances, nature, and even God for things which are the outer manifestations of our inner milieu. The life we live is a mirror of our values, drives, motives, and desires. Most of our anxieties are not the result of what life has done to us, but what we have done with life. The choices we have made, the associations we have developed, the time we have spent, the mate we have selected, the work we have done, are all determined by what's inside us. Trouble doesn't just happen; we get into a position, repeatedly, for it to happen to us.

Often certain kinds of people frustrate us because of unresolved tensions about that kind of person within us. And further, often the troublesome people of our lives have become the way they are because of what we do and say to them. We criticize and censure the very situations we ourselves have caused. However much we protest, the truth is that we have gotten into these situations, inadvertently, even habitually, and become involved in the multiplicity of activities we say we abhor, because of our inner equivocation. We get satisfaction from complaining, sublimation in accusing, and security in turbulence. Something or someone must be our culprit. But the truth of the matter is this:

43

we have made our own beds and our morning backache is no one's fault but our own! The Psalmist prayed, "Let the words of my mouth and the meditation of my heart be acceptable in thy sight." But that's just the rub! Our meditations are not acceptable. Only the pure in heart see and experience God's surprises.

But what is a pure inner self? The Greek word *katharos* has a variety of meanings, each of which suggests an aspect of what it means to have a pure heart.

It means cleansed and washed. A pure piece of material is clean. Our inner self is pure when it is washed clean of memories of past failures. We do not see God at work if we are blocked by impaired vision caused by unrepented and unforgiven mistakes of our lives. When we dwell on them, berating or justifying ourselves, then—unwittingly—the error itself becomes the goal of our imagination, and we repeat the same things and become defeated people. The first step toward a pure heart is to confess to God in the presence of a friend what we have done and accept the forgiveness offered to us. David prayed, "Create in me a clean heart, O God, and put a new and right spirit within me." Now listen to Jesus: "Neither do I condemn you; . . . go and do not sin again."

Two other uses of the word *pure* describe the next step. It is used for grain which had been sifted from all chaff or an army which was purged of malcontents, cowards, or the disobedient. This suggests that a pure heart is one in which the motives of life have been sorted out. No one has unmixed motives. Near the end of the French Revolution, Napoleon said in reflection, "Vanity made the revolution; liberty was only a pretext." What are the motives and pretexts of your life? Our most beneficent acts are colored by our selfish needs and desires. The legion of thoughts and attitudes which determine our life must be purged under the rigorous judgment of Christ. We must dare to ask, "Why do I do what I do?" and "What was my real motive in this?"

But how shall we decide? There must be some basis for the unification of our inner selves. This is found in a final use of the word *pure*. It is also descriptive of milk or wine which is unadulterated with water or foreign matter, or metal which has no tinge of alloy. It is undistorted and undiluted. A pure heart is single and simple; it is whole and undivided. That idea prepares us for the final step.

Søren Kierkegaard said that purity of heart "is to will one thing, and that is Christ." A person with a pure heart is no longer like John Bunyan's "Mr. Facing-Both-Ways." He knows a reunion of the divided and fragmented self. This results in a freedom from doubleness of mind in every sphere of life. The Psalmist prayed for purity of heart when he prayed, "Unite my heart to fear thy name." He urgently desired an unmixed condition of being. James spelled out to the early church the painful implications of impurity of heart: "For that person must not suppose that a double-minded man, unstable in all his ways, will receive anything from the Lord" (James 1:7-8).

The point of the fact is that we cannot receive what God has to give or see him at work in our lives because of the hypocrisy of our double mind. God is known not in mystical experiences or spiritual moods. He is a God of creative action. He commands and we must obey. He calls and we must follow. We "see" him only when we are involved with him in his continuing creation. In struggle and suffering, love and caring, giving and forgiving, we will be surprised by God. If we will to do his will as he reveals it to us, then we shall see.

45

Purity of heart is concentration of the whole personality upon God as the center of our lives. This is the opposite of the heart which wills everything, avoiding the necessity of making a choice among many appealing claims upon life. This inner ambivalence causes outer ambiguity. As Emerson said, "When simplicity of character . . . is broken up by the prevalence of secondary desires, and duplicity and falsehood take the place of simplicity and truth, the power over nature as an interpreter of the will is . . . lost."

This seems to be the same problem the Apostle Paul experienced in his struggle for purity of heart, recorded in Romans 7:7: "My conscious mind whole-heartedly endorses the Law, yet I observe an entirely different principle at work in my nature. This is in continual conflict with my conscious attitude, and makes me an unwilling prisoner." (Phillips)

How quickly Paul had forgotten his own advice to the Romans in Chapter 6: "You *belong* to the power which you choose to obey, whether you choose sin, whose reward is death, or God, obedience to whom means the reward of righteousness." (Phillips)

That's the answer! A radical choice within us must be made. Christ must become the central focus of our hearts. We must think of him, experience his healing of our emotions, and desire his will to be done in our lives. The result will be that we will actually become like him. This singleness of heart will affect the life we live. When we want to serve him, share his love, extend his ministry, we have a basis for the choices in the complexities of life.

"Problems! The one thing I don't need more of is problems!" a man shouted in response to my simple question, "How are things going?" Then he related what he called the "problems" of family and finances, children and job, pressure and worries. He is like most of us. Then we talked deeply about these "problems." Soon we got into what was going on inside him. There we found a complex of hopes, dreams, ambitions, and needs, pulling him in different directions. Near the end of the conversation we were able to see that he had never turned all these inner forces over to Christ. He was able to do just that. I checked on him the other day. The "problems" were beginning to diminish. "You know," he said, "I thought I had problems. Really I had only one—I had never given Christ complete control. Since I did that, I have had a different spirit about my difficulties. Now I can't wait to see what God is going to do with them!"

Leslie D. Weatherhead translated Psalm 59:10—"My God in his steadfast love will meet me"—in a very warm and reassuring way: "My God in his loving kindness, shall meet me at every corner."

We all face corners in life; none of us knows what's around the bend. Kierkegaard said, "What is anxiety? It's the next day!" We all need to know that the gracious God of forgiveness and new beginnings, of innovation and ingenuity, will surprise us with an uncalculated, undreamed of, unexpected way through the problems we face.

If we are teen-agers, God will meet us at the corner of career, morality, education, identity. If we are young marrieds, God will meet us at the corner of financial worries, a difficult child, a new job, a plateau of affection, or a breakdown of understanding. If we are at the corner of retirement, God will meet us with the challenges of continued usefulness and adventure in a second phase of life. If we are at the corner of sickness, God will be there with healing or the strength to glorify him even in pain. If we are at the corner of death, God will be there with the hope of eternity. Jesus never promised that it would be easy, but he did promise to be with us. "I am with you always, to the close of the age." (Matthew 28:20) Turn the corner by faith—he's there waiting for you!

All of this is rooted in the surprising God who "gives life to the dead and calls into existence the things that do not exist." What does this mean for practical experience of daily living other than that he is able to take our dead dreams, our diminished hopes, our tired bodies and give new life? What does this mean for impossible situations other than that there are possibilities God will reveal that we could not imagine could ever exist.

There is an excitement which I read on the faces of people who are living the serendipity of the sixth Beatitude. They have found a faith that works because God is at work. When they are tempted to despair, a letter arrives, a job is offered, a friend is sent to help, healing is given, a financial bind is broken by some unexpected resource, a home is found, a child begins to grow in insight and maturity, an unthought-of possibility comes into focus; and they are surprised. I believe that the Author and Architect of it all is delighted! He has a great cadre to deploy, circumstances to arrange, and powers to release, if we will only trust him. Jesus was right: "It is the Father's good pleasure to give you the kingdom." It is his inclination and will to work out what we thought were knotty problems of our life. He's for us and wants to use us to get his work done in the world. Not only does he meet us at the corners of life; he sets us free to become stationed at the corners of need in the lives of those who suffer personally or socially. But that will mean getting into trouble— for the right reason—in a life full of surprises.

6 / involved in trouble

Being a Christian means getting into trouble. This means something far more profound and creative than causing the trouble or being the trouble. It means that we are to be actively involved in peacemaking wherever there is misunderstanding, hostility, hatred, division, or conflict. I want to discuss what this means, really, and tell some stories of people who are contemporary peacemakers.

At the conclusion of the Beatitudes, Jesus staggered his disciples with such a vivid picture of their potentiality and his fantastic confidence in them that they could never again be satisfied with the safe, cautious lives they had lived. He told them that they were to share in God's eternal purpose of peace for all men and creation by being involved in his essential activity of reconciliation. They would experience God's nature and character as his sons and would be ranked among the prophets of old wth power to speak the truth in love in spite of persecution. The climax of the Beatitudes has been reached. Now this is where the action is! The joy of life as it was meant to be was to be found in an overt, propagative, initiatory involvement in the vortex of trouble.

We must clarify what Jesus meant by peace. We are as confused about it as were Jesus' listeners. He was careful to point out that there was a difference between his peace and the peace offered by the world. He said, "Peace I leave with you; my peace I give to you; not as the world gives do I give to you." The peace of the world was temporary, incomplete, and shallow. It was simply the brief, situation-oriented peace which was the result of cessation of present conflict between nations, groups, or people. It was the peace of appeasement and was not lasting because it had not resolved any of the essential issues of life or touched the core of man's deepest turmoil.

Jesus' peace was so different in source and extent that he said, "I have not come to bring peace, but a sword." What he seemed to be saying was simply, "Do not confuse my peace with victory over Rome or the mere cessation of battles through dominance over an enemy. My peace is much deeper than that." He went on in Matthew 10:35-39 to give a clarifying description of his mission. His peace would be possible only as a result of the experience of loving God above and beyond all the secondary loyalties of life. Peace would be the condition of mind and heart once a man lost his life for God's sake. For Christ it was not peace at any price, but at the highest possible price. He knew that no one could find peace until he loved God first with all his being. He did not say, "Now, now, don't worry—everything is going to be all right." Instead, he offered a peace which was the result of a resolution of the inner conflict between man and God.

Peacemakers are those who have had this kind of traumatic reorientation of their loyalties, motives, and values. The civil war within them is over. God's amazing grace has won their minds and hearts. Instead of fighting him, they are ready to do battle for justice in the world. They have learned that there can be no peace in the world until men know the peace of Christ. Growth in peacemaking is therefore progressive. It begins with this experience of peace through forgiving love, progresses out into our relationships, then becomes effective in helping others in conflict, and eventually must be focused in the grievance gaps of our society.

Every age has its particular centers of tension caused by the changes precipitated in that age. Ours is an age of gaps. These gaps in understanding become the locale of our peacemaking. Five, among many others, need our particular concern: the marriage gap, the generation gap, the racial gap, the opportunity gap, and the believability gap in the church. Here is where peacemakers are needed to listen, clarify, mediate, and open communication. If indeed the dividing walls of hostility have been broken down, then we are to show men and women that love and forgiveness can work. But how often we stand by and watch marriages dissolve, families living in discord, friendships estranged, and relationships strained! "It's none of my business," we say; or, "They would resent my interference." This says more about us than about the people in trouble. It says that we have not given ourselves in deep friendship and openness, expressing our own faith, which would make us the kind of people others will turn to in the difficulties of life.

Here is one way peacemaking works in the marriage gap. A couple was forced to face the terrible syndrome of mediocrity in which they lived—periods of tender love, followed by careless-ness, taking each other for granted, broken communications, and ending in open hostility which punctuated the long periods of silence. Then, when one or the other could take it no longer, he or she would break the bind temporarily, and a few weeks of tender love would flow again. But soon the syndrome would begin again, and they would go through the same process. This particular time it was more serious—neither was willing to go through the frustrating experience again, even if that meant separation. The breakthrough occurred when another couple, who had been through much the same syndrome but had received healing, was able to lay out their lives for the first couple to see. They shared what they had found and were able to help their friends face the hurt of the years and see how they were not meeting each other's needs. The purpose of God's healing the one marriage was so that this couple might be peacemakers for others. I know of dozens of couples whose lives are now filled with this demanding ministry to other couples.

There are few challenges in our time which need to be thought, talked, and prayed through more than this. Once we have, then God can use us as peacemakers in this growing problem in America. How many husbands and wives would be willing to work through this in order to be available to God as agents of peace in the troubled marriages all around us?

Whether you are a teenybopper or a fogybopper, the generation gap is more excruciating today than ever. Young people have exposed the mixed motives, distorted values, and imprisoning prejudices of the older generation. Older people and parents find the new morality, the emerging neuter sex with its long hair, flat chests, and unscrubbed faces, impossible to accept. As a father said, "The towel companies which used to make 'His' and 'Her' towels can anticipate the emerging generation and mark them all 'Theirs.'" A young woman explained her rebellion this way: "I don't feel my parents believe very much. At least, I don't see them making the hard choices which would apply their faith to social issues. I'm not sure what they want out of life—really." A college senior recently confided in me how very disturbed he was to realize how prejudiced his parents were. At a parents' weekend at his school he could feel their rejection of his black friends and their hostility to his date of another

INVOLVED IN TROUBLE

faith. "But they're the leaders of their church back home! How can they believe what they do and act that way?" Peacemaking comes alive in this context. How can we bridge the gap to help adults to be more consistent in belief and action and young people to discern the true values in their parents and accept them as fallible human beings? It's judgment that's tearing the generations apart.

An example of peacemaking in the generation gap is seen in a man who has lived through the ache of broken communication and eventual reconciliation with his avant-garde son. God showed him the way he had failed his son and caused much of the disturbing rebellion the boy expressed. The long nights of prayer, the rebuffed efforts to help, and the painful sense of failure were in preparation for peacemaking. Years after this man and his son were over their difficult years and they had become honest friends, the man was able to help a couple who were nearly insane with worry over their own son. I saw him the other day. He looked tired; yet he was joyous. He told me that he had been out all night looking for another couple's lad who had run away from home. He had found him and had helped him understand his parents. Then he had spent time with the parents to show them how to communicate love to their estranged son. That's peacemaking!

The racial crisis mounts. But it's not as simple as before. Black power is not white with purity, and the white world is not all black with prejudice. There is still a long way to go for white people to live out what is now the law in our nation, but the black must learn the responsible, nonviolent use of his growing power. Peacemaking in this crisis demands that we really believe that God has made us all one and that the dividing walls of housing, economics, job opportunity, and psychological as well

53

as physical differences mean nothing to God. We have all built the walls, and there are skilled masons, white and black, on both sides of the wall.

One woman found her peacemaking ministry with a black woman who had come to her community. They both had education, culture, and interests in common. The friendship grew, but so did the crisis in the black woman's life. She struggled to find her identity in a significant life. Because of her education and sophistication, she found the black ghetto impossible. She became emotionally disturbed through her sense of rejection by both blacks and whites. In it all, her friend ministered as a peacemaker, constantly trying to help this woman see her deep prejudice against the white community and her unwillingness to receive however little love she found. With each heartbreaking episode of adjustment, the white woman was there to help her talk it out. The terrible extremity of the cultural sickness became God's opportunity for healing because of a friend who cared.

If we are to live through this period of history in America, peacemaking must be accomplished on both sides of the wall of hostility. We need to follow Christ into this difficult, complex sociological problem and make peace through unemotional conversation and action when the specific opportunity for social change is presented.

But prejudice is not limited to the black revolution. A student foundation on a university campus made a grave mistake in room assignments. An Arab Christian and a Hebrew Christian were assigned the same room. Both believed in Christ but with very different ethnic backgrounds. I shall never forget the horrible cries of anguish which came from that room in the middle of the night. The two students were in a death grip expressing the anger each had for the other's nation. We tore them apart.

54

The eyes of both men were filled with terrible hatred. They had not expressed Christ's love, but prejudiced hostility. Only after days of intense counseling were those men able to see that Christ alone could make them one and help them see beyond the issues which separated them. The involvement in this conflict revealed to me that Christ alone is our peace and the key to personal and international crises. But the peacemaking took time and care—it stretched me and demanded all that I had.

The opportunity gap, centered in the problem of poverty and affluence, is another area for peacemaking. Most of our associations are with people of our own economic level. In addition to pressing ahead with litigation and programs to provide for the poor, we need to become involved with people who are underprivileged, to incarnate Christ's hope.

A man whom I respect very much sold his business and got involved in training dropouts and oppouts to use the tools of his trade. He has little in common with these men. Some are ex-convicts, others are drifters, while others are just undermotivated "leeches" on society. The job-training school at which he taught presented him with a tremendous opportunity for peacemaking. But he became distressed when he realized the cultural, spiritual, and motivational gap which existed between him and those people who were trapped in the poverty syndrome without vision or purpose. For a brief time he lived under the lie that the powers of evil were in charge and that the walls of misunderstanding were too high to climb over for any significant communication. Most of them could live just as well on their government subsistence check as work for a living—so why work? The man brought his need to a small prayer group of which he is a part. The group prayed for his release from judgment and prejudice. God's gift was one of deep inner peace and then the growing conviction that God was in control and the walls of separation were an illusion projected from both sides. The results were exciting. The classes changed and the communication of love from him was restored. The hope of a new life through Christ and specific training for a useful, industrious life are being given those men in need. That's peacemaking!

The challenge to study the peace and unity of the church which is shared by all Christians is no simple task in this day of church renewal. The church in America is fragmented between those who are pressing ahead with revolutionary changes in church life and those who yearn for the good old days. Should the church be involved in social issues? Should churchmen demonstrate? How can the church be relevant to the technological age? These questions are only the smoke which says there is internal fire. Churchmen are awakening to realize that their faith is a conglomeration of sixteenth-century garb, eighteenth-century customs, nineteenth-century theology, and ineffective moralisms. The church has lost its influence among large segments of our population. What shape will the contemporary church take to rediscover its ministry at a time like this?

It is in this believability gap that there is a need for peacemakers who are unreservedly committed to Christ and filled with his Spirit and who also are on the move to change society. The peace in the church will be maintained by those who know the biblical faith, love Christ, and are involved in communicating their faith to others, and yet are out on the frontier of community need. Only people who possess the best of the two worlds of personal faith and radical ministry will be able to speak to both sides of the conflict raging in the American churches.

There is an elder in a church in a metropolitan area who is an example of this. He knows Christ and lives under moment-by-moment guidance. As a mandate from his Lord, he felt that his church should take a stand on open housing. Because of who he was, he was able to challenge the conservatives and mediate with the liberals. The church remained united because of the peacemaker in a crisis which could have split the church.

The only hope for the church, our families, our friends, and our society is in the ministry of peacemakers. The reason we are alive and the reason the church exists in the world is to share the "peace which passes all understanding."

We must ask: What are the specific things we can say and do to bring clarification, insight, empathy, communication, and love? If we are honest, there are probably painfully practical things which we are under the Master's orders to do today. Most of the conflicts, personal and social, in which we are involved desperately need someone to break the bind in an expression of forgiving love. A peacemaker who has found God's peace is able to take the first step. He can do those things which express affirming love whether it is returned or not. He can admit his weakness and failure in the situation and do those things which will build a bridge of understanding. He is defenseless because, more than wanting his own way, he wants healing. It is more important to him to bring reconciliation than to be "right."

But it won't be easy. We will be misunderstood and rejected. We may get caught in the crossfire of hostility and hatred. We may be called everything from meddlers to opportunists. We may even be blamed for the very things we try to heal.

Our strength and security will be that it has ever been thus. There is no alternative for the Master's men. He told us we would have trouble in the world but to be of good cheer, for he had overcome the world. Believing that, we can go on getting into trouble—all the while rejoicing in a prophetic ministry.

❦ the purpose of life
as it was meant to be

7 / we are all ministers

"Well, frankly, I think you were a coward to leave the business world. You give the impression that the only place we can serve Christ is in church and that if I took Christ seriously, I would go into the ministry."

The pastor was stunned and shocked. He meticulously adjusted his carefully laundered clerical collar as if to remind his parishioner of his "sacred" calling. He tried not to show how disturbed he was, but anger blushed through his face. This prominent businessman in his congregation had touched a raw nerve. Something was wrong. The very people he ought to be able to reach were turning him off.

A couple of years before, this clergyman had been a successful businessman himself. He worked for a large oil company and lived in a lovely suburb. He had become active in his church and was pleased when the people asked him to become a church officer. Soon he became immersed in church work and blocked out other interests and concerns. He worked closely with his pastor and became a responsible churchman.

But he got the impression from his pastor that the highest calling for a Christian was to "go into full-time Christian service in the ministry." His job at the office became less challenging and interesting. He found it difficult to be a Christian there and became critical of the "inconsistencies and compromises of the business community." Finally, he became his pastor's pride and joy and the congregation's best "example" when he decided to leave the ambiguities of the business world behind and, though in his late forties at the time, go to seminary. The great goal of serving Christ "really" as a clergyman spurred him on. As he studied, the "holy" office became increasingly more important to him.

There was a great sense of accomplishment when he was ordained and called to his first church. No one ever looked or acted the part of a clergyman better than he did. He was filled with pious punditry, fulfilled all the images, and gave strong organizational leadership to his congregation. His great security was that he had sacrificed a career in business to "follow Christ." But no one appreciated his martyrdom! Out of insecurity, he overplayed the pastoral role. He was an eighteenth-century Scottish "dominie" in a twentieth-century American suburb. Confused, he redoubled his efforts. He built up the congregation in size and budget. Having uncertain goals, he initiated a building program which gave at least some of the members a sense of "being the church."

But underneath it all, he was lonely, afraid, and defeated. Because he thought he had to lead from strength, he did not dare to tell his people how he felt. In a few years he was a leader in his denomination, but he often had the same divided loyalties in the ecclesiastical world that he had felt in the business world.

This pastor told me his story at a clergy renewal conference at our church recently. The theme of the conference was "The Ministry of the Laity—a Key to the Renewal of the Church." Members of the laity spoke simply about their discovery of ministry in the world, beyond the local church. We talked honestly and openly about the things we do as clergymen to debilitate the renewal of the church. We faced false securities and phony clericalism. Then the conversations went to the heart of our personal need to rediscover the authenticating, humanizing love of Christ.

It was a dynamic week. The great discovery that my new friend made was that he was standing in the way of his church coming alive. He realized in a new way the biblical truth that all Christians are called to ministry in the world. The task of the church is to help Christians discover that they are ministers already and that all are in "full-time Christian service." The purpose of the church is to equip people for this ministry in the normal, natural situations of life.

This pastor went home a different man. The following Sunday he spoke with warmth and love about what he had rediscovered. Many of the congregation sensed the reality of his growing freedom and joined with him in sorting out the ministry which is given to the whole people of God. Now he is released to admit that he had cherished a false security of his office. This honesty has enabled his men to include him in on some very probing discussions of how they could live out their ministry in the business world. His church is on the move!

The great need in our time is not for more clergymen. Contrary to misguided opinion, most of the major denominations have more than they need. What we do need is more ministers: church members who realize that they have a ministry as servants of Christ in the homes, offices, factories, clubs, political parties, and social action groups. It is wrong for dynamic laity to be forced to feel that they must become clergymen to have a ministry. Strategic in the renewal of the church is the proclaiming, equipping, and enabling of the ministry of the laity.

In our church in Bethlehem, there are several staff enablers and potentially 2,100 ministers. We do not allow people to call the clergy "ministers." Our persistent question is, "What is the shape of *your* ministry, and what can we do to prepare and sustain you in your obedience?" Few things have done more to set our people afire and to radically alter our program as an equipping center for ministry in the world. The ministry can no longer be relegated to the clergy. Ministry is the function of all the followers of Christ and not the title of a few.

Confusion over ministry has caused a deep sickness in the contemporary church. We pedestal the clergy and demand of them an impossible role. We relegate the laity to innocuous games of playing church. The clergy become the paid gigolos of the congregation—spiritual lovers of people who will not love each other or the sick world Christ died to save.

Recently I watched a football game with my two boys. At a point of heated conflict over a referee's decision on a penalty, something ridiculous happened which portrayed too much of what is happening in the church today. The coaches of the two competing teams were out on the field arguing with each other and the referees while the players stood on the sidelines and cheered them on. That's like a clergy-oriented church! The paid professionals are out on the field while the members sit by and watch the performance. Can you imagine a game played by the coaches? About as absurd as many congregations!

On the chapel Communion table in the renewal community in Iona, Scotland, there is a chalice on which there is a disturbing inscription of a question which demands an answer each time it is used. It is Jesus' question to one of the disciples at the Last Supper: "Friend, why are you here?"

This is life's most crucial question. It is asked by our Lord in every situation and about our lives as a whole. Why are we here? What is our purpose?

Jesus says that we are to be perfect as our Heavenly Father is perfect. We are staggered by the challenge. How can anyone be as perfect as God? Who would ever dare even to try to measure up to that perfection?

The Greek word used to translate Jesus' word is *teleios.* This word does not mean abstract perfection. It comes from the noun *telos,* which means, end, goal, or purpose. It is used for anything which accomplishes the destiny for which it was created or fulfills the purpose for which it was intended.

Our purpose is to experience and express the reason we were given life: to minister. Jesus' statement was given at the conclusion of his delineation of how the life he had portrayed in the Beatitudes was to be lived out in the world. When we look over the admonitions which preceded this astounding challenge, (Matthew 5:13-47) we can understand the aspects of our purpose. We have been given the joyous quality of life we have considered in previous chapters, not for our pleasure alone, but to fulfill God's purpose.

We are to be secular saints, called and commissioned as ministers to live in this age, fully immersed in the world and unreservedly relevant. The word *minister* means servant. It was because God loved the world that he gave his love in Christ, and it is because of this same love for the world that he gives us to the world to continue Christ's ministry. We exist, not for ourselves, but for others. That's why we are here! The churches of which we are a part exist for those who may never darken their doors.

Jesus began the ministry of the laity in the Sermon on the Mount. He called nonprofessionals and entrusted them with tremendous responsibility. Those who found life as it was meant to be were to be the salt and light of the world. The more we grapple with what this means, the more the humble metaphors become reality for us, and the more we will comprehend the nature of our ministry.

Jesus' challenge is: "Get lost!" We are called to lose ourselves in the lives of others. We exist to season the lives of others. His statement that we are the salt of the earth must be combined with the statement, "He that findeth his life shall lose it: and he that loseth his life for my sake shall find it" (Matthew 10:39). The very nature of salt is that it will be lost—creatively or ineffectually.

The disciples were to picture themselves as the complex which contained salt. Their saltness would be lost—but how? They had been taught early in their lives that the substance they knew as salt would quickly become savorless in contact with the earth. That's just what Jesus wanted for them: contact with the earth in a dynamic way. Here the *earth* meant people, situations, and the nation of Israel. The disciples were to invest themselves in the bland, tasteless life of people in such a way that what they found would be transferred to others. They were to *lose* their saltness! How then were they to be salted? By fellowship with Christ. He alone would replenish the content of salt in their lives. They were to be ground into the "crucible of identification" and transfer their salt into the insipid gruel of the lives of others.

But, knowing all this, why is it that so few Christians are involved in ministry? In addition to the distorted images of the clergy, there is the distorted image of what it means to be a Christian today. The criticism of the world, not the gospel, has shaped what most Christians are today.

The result is a *hypocrisy in reverse!* This is not the hypocrisy of trying to be more than we are; it is the hypocrisy of trying to be less than we are. Hypocrites of the old order paraded their faith before men, while hypocrites of the new order deny their faith before men. Among many of us there is a new conspiracy of secrecy and silence about God and what he has done in our lives. We find it difficult to talk about our faith in authentic language as much as some others find it difficult to keep quiet. We are so sensitive to being placed in a category, so aware of the criticism and ridicule of our contemporaries and significant others at work or in community that we refuse to talk about the central hope of our lives or express our ministry. We get edgy and uneasy whenever the subject of faith occurs and quickly change the subject. We perpetuate the great lie that what we have and are is the result of our own skill and verve. We do not know how to share the fact that God is the source and sustainer of our lives without appearing to be like an evangelist giving a hard sell on the sawdust trail. We hide in the anonymity of normal churchmanship; we become critical observers but seldom are enthusiastic participants in sharing what we have heard, leaving ministry to the clergy. We know that what we have found is the answer to the needs of the people around us and of our troubled world, but we are afraid, silent, and cautious. Inadvertently we contribute to the same reverse in others. This is the bushel of reversed hypocrisy which hides the light we are to be in a dark world.

Jesus says: "Live! Let the light of your life—the manifestation of God at work in the painful, practical, personal areas of life— shine!" We ought to be living such a radiant life that it prompts the question, "Why are you the way you are?" and opens the way for a positive answer of what God has done. There's nothing more silly than the answer to an unasked question. That's witnessing of the lowest order. But there's nothing more powerful and contagious than the answer to a sincere question about the source of our quality of life. That's witnessing of the highest order. Then we can answer in an unreligious, unjudgmental way that will communicate life and, subsequently, the Light of the World. If we are not living in such a way that people are pressing us for our key to life, then we are not truly alive.

This challenges both the old and new hypocrisy. Our purpose as light in the world is to do good works—that exposes the hypocrisy of words without actions; but the reason for the good works is to glorify God—that exposes action without words of witness. The life we live is to be clearly identified in source and substance as God's work in us. There is no such thing as a secret, uncommunicated Christianity. Either the secrecy destroys our faith or our faith destroys the secrecy. A man with a conviction must do one of two things; as Robert E. Speer used to put it: "Change it or spread it. If it is not true, he must give it up. If it is true, he must give it away. He must propogate it if it is true or repudiate it if it is false."

A man on a business trip was complimented by a client on his spectacular advancement in his company. He simply replied radiantly, "I am very thankful for the gifts I have received." "What do you mean? You did it by hard work!" the client insisted. "Yes, that's true," he replied, "but the strength, wisdom, and love were gifts with which to work hard." Later that night over dinner the client pressed him further to know the source of the remarkable joy and confidence the man had. Quietly, simply, but powerfully, he told him what had happened to him after he had let Christ control his life. The result was a deep conversation that lasted into the night, and the client eventually took a new look at his own life. This businessman did not have to "go into the ministry" to have a ministry.

8 / when love is the motivation

"The greatest treason," wrote T. S. Eliot, is "to do the right deed for the wrong reason." This is the treason religious men have committed in every generation. Religion has been a distracting substitute for the ministry of the laity motivated by love throughout history. Actually, it motivates people to do the wrong thing for the wrong reason. Rites, rules, and regulations are developed and practiced on the assumption that man can reach, placate, and please God. The elaborate systems of religion erect diminutive gods which eventually become more important than the God they were established to serve, or the essential ethic of daily life they were legislated to develop. Self-justification, guilt, perfectionism, legalism, and pride become the motivations which flagellate the human spirit into obedience. Beneath it all is the fallacious assumption that we can be good enough for God to deserve his love and approval.

There is a United States Marine recruiting poster which appeals to a very basic desire in human nature. The poster depicts a handsome, virile young American in uniform. He is obviously the kind of dynamic person many young men would like to be. The words at the bottom of the poster spell out the corps' effort to elevate the image of their recruits. They appeal to the desire to excel and be superior. The arresting, impelling words are simple, but subtle: "Only if you are good enough!"

These words ought to be placed on a banner and flown outside most churches. They really placard the belief of most of us that we can be Christians and can minister to others "only if we are good enough." Ingrained in our thinking is the fundamental assumption that Christianity is a program of goodness, and if we can be good enough we will qualify to deserve God's approval and acceptance and be used by him in the world. The years of emphasis on being "good Christians" have had their toll. Psychological conditioning, Sunday school emphasis on ethics, and moralistic preaching, have all contributed to the equation that a "good" life equals the Christian life. We have made more clear what people are required to do than what they can be released to be. For most of us, Christianity is still a set of rules, a program of behavior, and a pattern of perfection. God has become a cosmic policeman checking our actions and tabulating our failures; the Christian faith has become a program of performance; and the church is now a center of judgment where we try to become more religious.

The result is that most of us fall into one of four categories. Some of us have tried to fulfill the demands of an impeccably good life and have done rather well at it, are proud of the fact, and wish others would do as well but have little motivation to help them. Others have tried to live up to the standards of someone's delineation of the good life but failed repeatedly with resultant self-incrimination and renewed commitments to do better, but with little satisfying result. Then there are some who have acknowledged that we can never be good enough to be Christians and have not only stopped trying, but are hostile to God and his self-righteous emissaries who try to improve us.

And lastly, there are those of us who couldn't care less, for we have observed the inconsistency of most Christians and have written off the faith as pleasant idealism but ineffective for life.

All these categories have one thing in common: they have missed the truth of what Christianity is all about and are acting out or reacting to a bold untruth. To correct this is one of the most pressing challenges before us today if the church is to be renewed and ministry enabled.

I talked to an alcoholic the other day who had been helped by Alcoholics Anonymous. When asked if he had been helped by the church, he said, "No, after all that I've done, I could never qualify to be a Christian." Later that same day I talked to another man who had the same spiritual problem—in reverse. He was in reaction to the challenge to commit his life to Christ. "Why, I've been a good man and a fine Presbyterian all my life! Why is it now necessary for me to commit my life to Christ just in order to join this church?" Both men were hung up on "goodness-oriented Christianity." One disqualified himself on what he had not done; the other thought he qualified himself on what he had done. Both missed the point.

The difficulty of seeking to be good enough was the problem of the Pharisees. They punctuated Jesus' ministry with their criticism and hostility. They were the forefathers of contemporary "good Christians." They incarnated the belief that man was responsible to order his life in respectability. They had tried to spell out to the last detail the specific implications of the dictates of the Ten Commandments. In answer to the question, "What do these laws mean for everyday life?" they had written a code of rules which had been handed down through the years. Each generation of legalists had annotated the detail of the previous generation. The result was thousands of little regulations for every imagined detail of life. The Pharisees were the caretakers of these laws. They were the respectable citizens, the patriots, the pillars of Jewish tradition.

In this context Jesus seems all the more astounding—"For I tell you, unless your righteousness exceeds that of the scribes and Pharisees, you will never enter the kingdom of heaven."

We can only imagine how shocking this must have been to both Jesus' disciples and the Pharisees themselves. What he said was aimed at both groups. He wanted to expose both what the Pharisees were not and what the disciples could be. For all of them, as God's children, he yearned for the same thing: to have them enter the kingdom of heaven. This is the realm of God's rule, fellowship with God based on his love and forgiveness, and a life lived in gracious acceptance of and costly service to others. He introduced a new level of righteousness which would exceed, "overflow," in a joyous, nonreligious faithfulness and obedience to God in all of life. The disciples could have missed this because, like many of us, they probably felt that they could never be as good as the Pharisees, and the Pharisees, also like many of us, could have missed it because they were self-satisfied. Jesus pointed both groups to a quality of life which exposed both the false reservation of one and the false respectability of the other. The same is true today. The reluctant disciples and the proud Pharisees are still with us.

Love is the key word which describes the righteousness which exceeds the Pharisees in any day. The law given by God to Moses outlined clearly God's requirement of love and reverence to himself and those around us. The first half of the Decalogue deals wth a man's relationship with God, and the other half with his relationship to other people. Jesus made it very clear that he had not come to *destroy* this law, but to *fulfill* it. In fact, he was more deeply concerned about the law in its deeper intent than were the Pharisees. He called them back to the prior claim of God's original intention which had been lost in the religious particularism of little laws. Anyone who honestly tried to live by the Commandments was immediately aware of his own inadequacy and need for forgiveness. This was exactly what the Pharisees avoided and just what Jesus came to fulfill. "For the law was given through Moses; grace and truth came through Jesus Christ." (John 1:17.) He is more concerned about the law breaking our pride than our breaking the law. He knows that we who think we can be good enough for God have never come to grips with the Ten Commandments. We have never looked deeply at the inner attitudes and motives which contradict our outer religiosity.

In subsequent passages of the Sermon on the Mount he takes several of the Commandments and shows us how we have broken them in thought and feeling within ourselves. Perhaps we have not murdered, but we have destroyed people with depreciating words of anger, condemnation, and gossip. We may not have committed adultery, but what of lustful thought and dream? Or we may never have tolerated the thought of divorce, but what of the divorced spirit in marriage which frustrates and disturbs? Then too, we may never have sworn, but what of the lack of integrity through overstatement and verbal ebullience? Or take the sayings on resentment and retaliation. Hebrew ethics permitted just retaliation. Jesus went deeper than that with his cutting, "But I say unto you . . ." It was as if he were saying, "You are proud of your justice in regard to retaliation; now I tell you, you shall not retaliate at all!"

The message on turning the other cheek carries a deeper meaning than meets the casual reading. Picture what he is saying.

If a right-handed man stands in front of a man and tries to slap him, he will most naturally slap the left cheek with the palm of his hand. To turn the other cheek after that would be to offer someone an opportunity to slap the right cheek. This would require the back of the hand, and this, according to rabbinic law, is twice as insulting. Jesus suggests the most demanding kind of nonretaliation. We not only startle and amaze the persecutor, we force him to think about what he is doing. We say in substance, "If insulting me in these petty ways gives you some strange satisfaction, here, really insult me. It won't break my love for you either." The rules of the Pharisees had done just the opposite. The very term "Pharisee" means separated one. Jesus incarnated inclusiveness and involvement. He called men to live in such moment-by-moment sensitivity to God's Spirit that they would live in the situational guidance the Spirit gave for each new circumstance.

When we accept that we cannot be good enough, there is a profound humility which begins to grow within us. We exceed the Pharisaical spirit because we know that however far we have come in our growth, we still have so far to go. Yet it is within the context of Christ's accepting love that we grow. We do not press on in our development as people in order to earn God's approval but because we already are accepted and loved. That's freedom from religion!

The rich young ruler addressed Jesus as "Good Master." Jesus reacted to this projection of the young man's self-image. What he was really saying was, "You are one of my kind, Master. What does a good man like us do to be saved?" Jesus pressed him beyond concern for goodness. "There is none good but God. Why do you call me good?" Then he dramatically touched the area of the man's need. He thought he was good but was debilitated by his riches. Goodness was a self-conscious irrelevancy for Jesus. It was an indication that a man still was centered on the perpendicular pronoun. Jesus pressed him to obedience motivated by love.

What a relief it is to know that we shall never be good enough! This does not release us to slovenly mediocrity. Instead, it puts the focus where it belongs—on Christ. His grace is the only source of true goodness. We need neither reject the Christian faith because we are not good enough, nor take pride in the fact that we are, in our own judgment.

Let's change the banner, for the church at least, from "Only if you are good enough" to "Only if you are willing." The church is not a religious organization of good people; it is a society of sinners, changed and motivated by love. Do we qualify?

9 / the joy of sexuality

Recently in a popular magazine sex was used in a clever way to sell men's sport coats. A lovely woman, sparsely clad by only the folds of the sport coat, was curled up with a seductive look on her face. The caption (the only printing on the page except the manufacturer's brand name) was simply, "Man's second best ego-builder." The implication leaves little to the imagination. The problem, however, is that many have found that neither the coat nor the misuse of a woman is the answer to ego needs.

We live in a sex-centric society in which we face the real danger of distorting our sexuality. If we are to discover life as it was meant to be, there are few things which demand our thoughtful concern and Christ-guided understanding more than an authentic sexuality. Young and old, married and unmarried, widowed and spinstered alike, need to affirm and creatively express the dynamic of sexuality.

This is no simple matter in our time. No period of history has been more drenched with sex than ours. We are overinformed about some aspects of its physiology and yet know little of its profound mystery; we are overstimulated about its potentiality and are often let down when it is not the answer to all our needs; and we are oversold on its manipulative power and have tried to use it as a substitute rather than a sacred means of communication. Sex is no longer on the taboo list for polite conversation. Children are taught its physical intricacies in school, and there are informative articles about it in almost every edition of the popular magazines. Yet most people are unable to cope with the problems of their sexuality.

Our fears, fantasies, and frustrations, which we would be mortified to admit to anyone, are brashly used and confused by mass-media hucksters hawking their wares. Our sex drives are wrenched from our sexuality and used to sell everything from galoshes to garden tools, medications to mattresses, sporting goods to shaving soap, detergents to deodorants.

We are bombarded with erotic stimulants in entertainment and most forms of contemporary literature. Our feelings are manipulated in every waking moment. The sexual ethos permeates our thinking and attitudes. The question, however, which aches to be answered, is: "Are we any better prepared to express our sexuality in a healthy way?"

Some say yes. We are experiencing what is called the second sexual revolution. The 1920's broke out of the negation of sex, and today we are struggling to express sex in a new morality. Situational sex is now "in" for a larger number of people than we want to recognize. They chant the new ethic of Ernest Hemingway's manifesto: "What is moral is what you feel good after; and what is immoral is what you feel bad after." The dynamic, but not the danger, of sex as an end in itself is championed by an increasingly large number of young (and not so young) adults who have conditioned themselves to feel good after sex as an easily controllable exercise of pleasure with little thought of continuing relationship or responsibility.

A new code has emerged, based on the individual, subjective

perception of what is good in each given situation. But what is good—and by whose standards? What are the guidelines? Take the powerful ingredients of rebellion, search for identity, need for love, and insecurity; season them with social and group pressure, release them with the "pill" and charge them with the natural fires of passion, and you have the explosion of the sexual revolution. The lingering frustration of the new morality, however, is the old nature. Though the straitjacket of fear, religious codes, and moralisms has been unbuckled, we have provided little to guide people in developing a sane, integrated sexuality.

But what about the straight society of "mature" adults? Serious surveys, penetrating conversation, and honest confession of an amazingly large number of people indicate that for all our preoccupation with sex, it is still a major source of confusion, fear, and guilt. It is a major cause of marital maladjustment. Far too many of us simply have never learned to enjoy our sexuality in a genuine way and to admire and appreciate the sexuality of others. Though most of us would not be guilty of breaking acceptable social standards of what is proper, we are aware of our sexual needs and often relegate to the world of thought and imagination what we would never dare to admit in the open. We think that we alone are troubled when in fact almost everyone deals with feelings, attractions, and attitudes with sexual overtones which cause disturbance within. We cannot be disembodied! Our attitude toward our bodies and those of other people affects our feelings toward them. Some of us are still ashamed of sex, others of us are afraid of our sexual impulses, others are disquieted by our sexual thoughts, and still others are hampered and inhibited in any effort to be objective about our feelings. The result is guarded detachment, an ill-at-ease tenseness, or a psychological withdrawal from relationships of depth on the purely

76

social levels of life. Or perhaps our uneasiness manifests itself in a boisterous, overemphasis on sex in conversation, jokes, and fraternization. However, the root problem is the same: we are uncomfortable in our sexuality.

In Jesus' statement on adultery and lust in the Sermon on the Mount, he gives us the key for the discovery of Christian sexuality. "You have heard that it was said, 'You shall not commit adultery.' But I say to you that every one who looks at a woman lustfully has already committed adultery with her in his heart." (Matthew 5:27-28.)

He pressed deep into the inner realm of thought, feeling, and motive. He shocked his proud listeners by the admonition that adultery of the mind was as serious as adultery in fact. The ancient commandment on adultery had been a bulwark against the disintegration of the family. Now Jesus gave them a bulwark against the disintegration of inner character.

In a world of sensuality Jesus identified lust as the fount of distorted sexuality. Lust was the inner source of the fragmentation of sex from total personality. Adultery in fantasy or act would usually result. The pungent truth here is that lust makes a person a thing, an object of our desires. It thinks first of its own desire with little thought of the value and needs of the other person. It attaches itself in leech-like contact in thought and enjoys an aspect of a person apart from the whole. Jesus knew that no person had been created to be the object of selfish pleasure. He proclaimed the essential truth that joy could be found only in self-giving, not self-gratification. Sex, in Jesus' view, could not be isolated. People are not playthings, but dynamic complexities. This is the reason that when the woman taken in adultery was brought to him by her self-righteous accusers, his ire and indignation was focused on the accusers, not on the

77

accused. They could not respond to his challenge to cast the first stone, because they too were guilty, inwardly. He seemed to be saying that lust to some degree is a universal problem of all of us. He penetrated to inner lust because he knew that it was there that authentic sexuality was confused in eroticism—enjoyment without relationship. Because a person had not come to a realization of the holy wonder of his own sexual nature, he would lustfully distort another person in thought.

The antidote to lust is love—for one's self as loved by God and for another as a gift from God. In the context of Jesus' affirmation of life in all dimensions we sense his desire to call men to a higher level of thought and expression of the gifts of sexuality.

Sexuality is the totality of our manliness and womanliness. It is personality in expression of thought, word, action, toward the opposite sex. It is not just the procreative capacity, genital desire or gratification, or simply the distinctive quality of the two sexes. The word *sex* was first used by the Romans. We first find it in the writings of Cicero. The word is derived from the Latin word *secare,* to cut or sever. It is traced back to the Greek fable that human beings were originally bisexual, until punished by Zeus with separation into male and female. Not so! We believe sexuality is a gift, not a punishment. God has made us male and female, not just for the perpetuation of the species, but as distinct expressions of his love, of value in and of ourselves. Human beings are superior to the animal world in that physical sex is an expression of total sexuality in mind, emotion, and body. Sexuality is a dynamic force which enables personality to attain its purpose of existing with and for others. We are born with this capacity. It is expressed in infancy and childhood in the bonds of family love; it grows in self-giving reciprocal relationships with friends and comrades of both sexes, and becomes the driving power of creativity, concern, and empathy in adult life. Sexuality is not merely a physical drive, but a profound mystery rooted in the human spirit. Lust alone pulls it out by the roots and feasts upon it apart from its context of wholeness.

Our sexuality is wonderful. It is beautiful to behold in both men and women. A woman who can sing, "I enjoy being a girl!" or a man who can sing, "I love life and I want to live" are exciting manifestations of God's creation to be enjoyed as much as a breathtaking scene in nature. A human being, pulsating with physical and spiritual beauty, is to be adored as part of the wonder of life. We are alive to affirm our humanity—to take sheer delight in our sexuality. There is nothing wrong, inferior, or evil in a lovely body, a charming countenance, or a warm attractiveness. We are stewards of our nature, and we are to thankfully express praise to our Creator for the joys of being men and women. The attractiveness of another's body, the radiance of his or her face, the tone of voice, the touch of gesture, the challenge of mind, are all inseparable aspects of appreciating the sexuality of those around us. Lust will always fill the vacuum created by the absence of these powerful dynamics. It will be our undeniable danger signal that we have begun again to violate another's personality and have made an object of him.

Jesus suggested radical surgery. In vital hyperbole, he says: "If your right eye causes you to sin, pluck it out and throw it away; it is better that you lose one of your members than that your whole body be thrown into hell" (Matthew 5:29). What this means for us is—recognize the seriousness of the problem for what it is, confess your need, get it out into the open so that it can be healed by God. Lust can breed only in the dark chambers of the mind. Open the windows of the soul—let his love for you, and through you to others, flow in. Once we are yielded as a channel of his love, lust will be burned up in a purifying fire. The result will be a mature, Christian sexuality.

But adultery of the mind is as destructive in marriage as outside. We can live together and use each other without concern for the total self as much in the sacred bonds of marriage as with a chance association. The complex needs of a person can be neglected.

Sex can be used as a weapon to control and as a reward in a game of reciprocity. As Katherine Whitehorn said, "Sex is a natural force, like fire; and like fire, it can weld or warm or it can destroy." The problem arises when we think too much of our own needs and too little of the other's fulfillment. When patience, gentleness, and sensitivity replace lust, then mutual tenderness has begun. Sex is so pervasive and so intrinsically connected with every aspect of personality, that it cannot be separated from life as a whole without impoverishing the whole marriage. The wondrous gift of sex is given for two people in marriage to become one in spirit, mind, and body—and in that order! It is an expression of love, not the basis of it. When it becomes too crucial to one or unimportant to the other, it is out of focus. *Time* magazine was right: "The Victorians who talked a great deal about love knew little about sex. Perhaps it is time that modern Americans who know a great deal about sex once again start talking about love." [1]

I talked to a man at a conference who was deeply troubled by his thought life. After several hours of talking around his problem, he finally blurted out, "Well, my real problem is that I don't know what to do about my thoughts about women. I am happily married and yet I find that I am constantly thinking the

---

[1] *Time,* January 24, 1964, p. 59.

wrong things about other women. It has inhibited and frustrated my relationships." We talked at length about the source of this. He had never thought of joyously appreciating women as a gracious gift to be reverently cared for as a gift from God. I suggested that each time a thought of lust occurred, he pray something like this: Holy Father, thank you for this child of yours. Thank you for all the aspects of her personality. Thank you for making me responsible for her, to express loving concern for her as a whole person.

I received a letter from this man recently. This is what he said: "I am just amazed at what has happened to me. I have never been freer or more relaxed. I have come to a profound praise to God for women. It has begun a new relationship with my wife and a healthier view of my attitude toward all women. My thoughts are filled with praise. Thanks for the secret."

10 / marriage is for loving

It was still dark at 6:30 A.M. one winter morning when a large group of our men gathered in the church fellowship hall for the Tuesday morning breakfast. There was good fellowship around the tables as the men ate and discussed the theme of the morning, which was marriage, based on Jesus' teaching in the Sermon on the Mount. As we considered the passage, we realized that Jesus was dealing with a much more significant question than rules about divorce. He was really pressing the question, "What does God intend marriage to be?" It was this deeper question which I tried to answer in a talk which began at 7:00 A.M. sharp. I had no idea the disturbance the questions I finished with would cause before that day was over. I asked,

Are you more in love with your wife than you were when you courted; than you were ten years ago—last year—last week? If you had something to share which was exciting and crucial to you, is your wife the first person with whom you would want to share it? Would she understand? Would she share your enthusiasm?

In your sexual life, do you find your wife more attractive, your union more satisfying, and the ways of romance more adventuresome than ever before?

82

Do you anticipate going home at night after work? Whom do you look forward to seeing most—your wife, the children, or the dog? With what kind of an intonation does your wife announce, "Dad's home"—a question mark, an exclamation point, a semicolon, or a drab period?

If you could choose any woman in the world to spend a weekend of fun and frolic with in New York, would you choose your wife?

What's the one thing you could do today to communicate unselfish love to your mate? What would you say or do to communicate to her that you want to keep your romance alive?

The questions caused a great stir. There were mixed reactions on the men's faces. Some smiled, others laughed, and many had a twinkle in their eyes. But there were others who were deadly serious because the questions had exposed their need. They were forced to see their marriages as they were and were counting the cost of communicating unselfish love. They seemed unsettled by the answers they had given within their own minds.

We declared that day "Just Because Day." We committed ourselves to do the practical, maybe silly, little or grand, overlooked or resisted, thing which would spell initiative love or forgiveness, if need be. We were determined to do it, just because of love—Christ's love for us and our love for our mates. I could tell by the look on the faces that each knew what that one thing was.

At 7:30 A.M. I finished my talk, and the men were off to work. Some lingered afterward to talk. Many of them confessed to me that they had not done very well in answering the questions and had to admit that there was little excitement left in their marriages. None was on the verge of divorce or in deep marital trouble or scratching the seven-year itch, but romance seemed to have been lost as the years had flown by.

A few hours later, after the men had gone to work, I gave the same talk and asked these same questions at a morning coffee hour sponsored by the Women's Association. The wives of many of the men with whom I had breakfast were there. I simply changed the gender of the questions and developed the talk about marriage from a wife's point of view. The questions caused the same uneasiness as they had earlier. The obvious question on every wife's face was, "How did my husband answer?"

What a day that turned out to be! Many of the couples shared with me what happened that night when the men came home from work. Some of the men brought home flowers or a little gift which had secret significance to their wives. Others went about doing the thing which had been put off for months or even years! And others started conversations about things which had been buried in hostility for too long.

The wives had been preparing during the day, also. Some of them greeted their husbands with a warmth, tenderness, and enthusiasm which had been lacking for years. One woman had her hair done, changed her dress, and was waiting for her husband at the door when he came home from the office. She knew how much this meant to him but had refused to do it previously until he changed some things which bothered her. Another had called the travel agent and started plans for a trip which she had put off taking with her husband.

There is not space to recount all the amazing things which took place on that "Just Because Day." But the conversations that evening were very telling. Some edged into the subject gradually, while others barged into it boldly. In most homes, however, the question was finally asked, "Well how *did* you answer those questions this morning?" One man, in affirmation of his wife, laughed and said to her, "By the way, how would you like to spend a weekend in New York with me alone? Don't tell your husband! Let's just go off together!"

The thing I learned anew that day was that for many people the joy has been lost in their marriages and they need some way to begin again. As one man asked, "If you have lost exciting love in your marriage, how do you regain it?"

I believe that this is just where many Christians find themselves in marriage. Because two Christians live in the same house does not make it a Christian marriage. The more I talk with people about their faith, the more I realize that one of the most difficult places to live out faith is in marriage.

We get hung up on oughts and images at this point. We know we "ought" to be different—more loving and less critical, or more or less whatever we know is needed. Self-reformation and promises eventually bog down. We have a false image that Christian marriage is where there is no conflict, argument, or difficulty. Or we picture a serene atmosphere of daily prayer, worship, and Bible reading, where the wife is submissive, the husband is the priest of his home, and where the children honor and obey out of love for Christ. But most of us are not there and hardly know where to begin. If we were to scrap all the images and standards and really wanted the unique style of family life Christ desires to give to each couple, where would we begin?

There are four things which work for me. I have not always had a Christian marriage. It was several years after I had become a Christian and had been in the ministry for some time that Mary Jane and I discovered Christ together in our marriage. These four steps mean everything to us now, and often we have to go back over them when communication breaks down.

1. *Begin with yourself.* The only person you have a right to change is yourself. A wonderful thing happens when we take the focus off what's lacking in the other person and dare to pray, "Lord, show me what you want me to be in this marriage. Give me power to love as you love me." Make a list of the things you receive in prayer that you need to change.

Praying like that is costly. Our Lord may tell us some things about ourselves that we perhaps would rather not face. There may be things we are doing which are keeping our marriages deadlocked in mediocrity. Difficulties in marriage don't just happen. They develop over a period of time. There are stages through which most of us have passed.

Some of us can remember the honeymoon stage when romance was dynamic and alive. Those were great days of discovery, adventure, and fun. All signals were "Go!" and the dreams of the future stretched out with hope and anticipation before us. No obstacle seemed too high; no problem too serious. Cramped living conditions, a tight budget, and personal adjustments were part of the challenge of beginning life together.

But then—when did it happen?—most of us were ushered into the next stage. We stopped "playing house" and settled down to the business of living. We got serious about getting ahead and began scrambling for the symbols of success. In this stage the two worlds of home and the job were wrenched apart, and most of us began living with the responsibilities of life in our separate worlds. A woman becomes involved and often exhausted in her multiplicity of demanding duties as mother, cook, maintenance expert, car pool driver, counselor, PTA leader, community worker, and—if there is time and energy left—a wife.

At the same time the husband is preoccupied in his world of work. His world is an extension of his ego which must be satisfied by progress and advancement. He too is engulfed in the tides of life's demands, pressures, and worries. His wife and family become a part of his life and no longer the central focus of his life.

It's at this point that identity problems begin. A woman begins to question who she is. The heroine of the family story, as a separate self and the subject of the drama of life, is lost in the endless subplots of togetherness. She feels she exists only for and through her children and husband. The Victorian culture did not allow women to accept and gratify their sexual needs, but our culture does not permit a woman to accept or gratify her basic need to grow and fulfill her potentiality as a person. As one woman said to her husband, "Your life is like a puzzle with a piece missing, and that piece is me. But I don't fit somehow. There was a time when the whole puzzle was put together around us. Now I feel like just a piece that needs to be cut to size to fit into the place you and the children have cut out for me. Oh, I know you all couldn't get along without me, but all I am is part of your life—necessary, but just a part."

Many men who stopped courting their wives long ago need to wake up to what has happened to their wives over the years. Some think that consistent sex and a little verbal affection ought to satisfy their wives' need for identity. Subtly, a wife becomes the object and not the person of her husband's affections. The things he did to win her seem silly and a bit adolescent for busy married couples. He becomes alarmed only when he is cut off and his wife is reluctant to fit into the changing shape of the missing piece of the puzzle of his life. He becomes insensitive to warning signals. He talks but does not communicate; he listens but does not hear. As long as she is that wonderful combination of lover, mother, helpmate, and cheerleader, he is satisfied—and negligent.

In some marriages the process is reversed. Many women become careless and neglect the very things which made them attractive to their husbands. They forget that men are often little boys at heart and need support and encouragement for the battle of life. There is nothing a man will not do for a wife who knows how to keep alive the tenderness of assuring love. No one can be taken for granted. Often a woman will fight for her identity with the very sharp weapons of rejection and reserve. Inadvertently she does what the husband has done. In her search for identity she allows her life to become overinvolved and he becomes a facet of her life.

Sound familiar? What is Christ saying to you about your marriage? What would he change if you would dare to begin with yourself?

2. *Be vulnerable.* That means being absolutely honest with your mate. Tell him or her anything which has been unspoken or unforgiven. Clear the slate and clean out the garbage. Be careful here: you are to be honest about yourself. This is not the time to air gripes about the other person. That's coercive. If your honesty is authentic, your mate will be encouraged also to be honest. Confess your own patterns which frustrate your marriage and ask your mate to help you change. Open yourself completely.

3. *Accept the uniqueness of your mate.* Most people get married for just one reason: to live with the person they love. But ever since Adam, the problem has been how to do it. The difficulty is that we seem to become aware of all the things about the other person which we dislike and wish he or she would change. Because we are all different, we face the crisis of dissimilarity. Nowhere else but in marriage are we exposed as we

88

are in our self-centeredness, stubbornness, and pride. No one knows us like our mates!

As one man said, "Getting married to my wife is like buying an old house. It will do for now, but I have some refurbishing and alterations in mind!" How many of you can say that you are completely satisfied with your mate just as he or she is? Don't answer too quickly! If you could change five things about your mate, what would you change? Did your mind race to any?

Criticism, which is motivated by the lack of fulfillment, becomes justified in the inadequacies of the other. We become amateur (if not amateurish) psychologists and analyze our mates as if some new insight will suddenly liberate them to be what they ought to be (which is usually written in our hidden agenda). Without a calculated decision of meanness anyone can drift into a conditional kind of love which hangs like a carrot before the mate's nose. Guilt over never measuring up and uneasy anxiety which comes from lack of "in spite of" acceptance begins to choke out the natural, free-flowing affection and permissive love we once felt but somehow lost.

Until we come to the point of accepting our mates just as they are and are willing to love them if they never change, we cannot discover the new dimension Christ has to give. We must cut the strings of our control and our guilt-inducing images. There is a sacred uniqueness in all of us which must be honored and nurtured in marriage. Our responsibility is to give affirming love, not change our mates. In the atmosphere of total acceptance a person is liberated to take a look at himself and desire to change. This desire is Christ's gift, but it is mediated through our acceptance.

4. *Be initiative.* Feelings follow action, not action feelings. Most of us sit around waiting for the right mood feelings so that

we can act the way we should. We analyze our attitudes and think that if we finally get the key to a relationship, we will feel differently. Not so! Do the thing which love demands and you will begin to feel differently. What would communicate love in language and action your mate will understand and appreciate? Don't wait. Do it for Christ's sake! Whether it means offering affection, saying you're sorry, doing some task, or being quiet long enough to listen, you must be the initiator.

Our danger at this point is that we rationalize ourselves out of responsibility. Often hostilities settle on silly, inconsequential issues. The deeper tensions are sublimated into some little thing which grows to have profound meaning. We become defensive and resist doing this very thing because it means giving in and accepting the dominant will of another person.

I know a man who could well afford a tailor to alter his clothing. In fact, he could buy a new suit each time one needs repair. Yet he insists that his wife must do these repairs. For him, it is an expression of caring; for her, it's a nuisance. He came home the other evening to find that his pants which he had asked to be repaired were untouched by his wife, who always found some excuse in her busyness. He was hurt and angry. He wanted caring to be expressed on his terms. These pants are not the issue in that troubled marriage, but they have become the focus. Initiative love for that wife begins with a needle and thread! But it does not stop there!

Or I think of a woman who needs expressions of affection in particular words and actions. Her husband, who thought she was overweight, was determined not to love her in the way she demanded until she reduced. She was disturbed and nibbled her way to greater obesity, saying, "If he loved me, I would reduce." Love for one meant loving affection, while for the other it meant control of weight. The husband was able to affirm her by loving her, obese as she was. When she could no longer focus her hostility on him as an excuse, she had to face her unhealthy weight.

Christian marriage exists when we become Christ's love incarnate to our mates. That means the cross: death to ourselves, our plans, and our patterns of manipulation. That happens when we turn our marriage, all that it is and could be, completely over to Christ and thank him that he is now in charge. Since he is Lord of the marriage, tell him how you feel. Be specific about your resentments, hurts, disappointments, broken dreams. Ask for and accept his forgiveness. Trust that he does live in you and will love through you.

I hope the Florists' Association does not capitalize on our idea of the "Just Because Day." They might make it a national holiday. But if other families could discover what some of ours did, it would be worth it. Marriage is for loving "just because" of Christ's unchanging love.

11 / the gift of words

The following statements and several others like them were made to me in the span of a few hours one day. They reminded me of how hard it is for people to put into words what they believe in order to help someone else.

"My son's in real trouble. I can't get through to him! If you could talk to him I know you could straighten him out. He needs some purpose, some meaning in his life. Will you talk to him?" the concerned father pleaded.

"There's a man at work who's facing some complex problems. I wonder, if I arrange a lunch for the three of us, will you talk to him?" asked a businessman who was becoming aware of the needs around him.

"My husband and I aren't communicating very well. If you could stop by and talk to us, maybe it would help," a worried wife confided.

"Since my neighbor's wife died, he's been in a real deep depression. We've had him over a lot lately, but find it's difficult to share with him what we believe about death. Will you make a call on him?" asked a believing but inarticulate church member.

"I didn't know what to say! In the middle of the cocktail

THE GIFT OF WORDS

party this woman began to tell me about some very personal problems she was having. I could tell that what she needed was God's love, but I just couldn't put into words what I had found in my faith to be of some help to her. I told her about our church and made her promise that she would come hear you next Sunday," said a woman who missed a tremendous opportunity to talk about her faith.

Each of these people quoted above has been active in the church through the years, but had to admit his dumbness when an articulare sharing of the faith was required by someone in need. Their words were not trusted—by them or others.

Jesus was concerned about words and cut to the core of one of the major causes of the breakdown of communication. He attacked duplicity in any form. He saw that men used words to pretend to be something outwardly which they were not inwardly in their inner selves. He heard words used to hide, camouflage, distort, manipulate, and impress. His world was no different from ours: words had been wrenched from reality and were spoken carelessly. Eventually, he was hung on a cross because of the clever use of words out of context by those who had evicted God from their lives and others who evaded the truth he spoke. When we take Jesus' words about oaths seriously, we see that words are a gracious gift for communication rooted in communion. They are equipment for ministry. For Jesus, words were sacred, sacramental, and solidifying.

What do you say when you want someone really to believe and take seriously what you have said? Note carefully the powerful adverbs which we use to prelude something which we want to be sure is heard and accepted as distinctly true and particularly significant. We say: Seriously now . . . What I honestly mean . . . Frankly . . . What I *really* mean . . . If you want it straight from the shoulder. Sound familiar? But were we not serious, honest, frank, true, direct, and sincere before? The impression these attention-getting, demarcation devices create is that what has been said before is not worthy of serious consideration.

Others of us use sacred words and institutions to alert our listeners to the importance or veracity of something we are going to say. If we want to stress a point or press others to say something, we say: For heaven's sake, listen . . . I swear it's true . . . For God's sake . . . believe me . . . Heaven strike me dead if I am not telling the truth.

All these expressions are indicative of a deep need in all of us to be heard, understood, and believed. Turn on the antenna! Pick up the signals people are sending in most conversation. We will hear the tremendous need to have communication most people express. We all want to break the sound barrier and register on another person's mind what is important to us. But these demarcation devices to alert people show that we want to be taken seriously but find words insufficient. We suspect words— our own and others' alike!

This is what Jesus was getting at in his challenge that words were sacred. Words of conversation, promise, and agreement had lost their sacredness and men relied on oaths to be sure of the integrity of another man's speech. The proud Jews who listened to Jesus had impeccably observed the third and ninth commandments: "You shall not take the name of the Lord your God in vain"; . . . "You shall not bear false witness . . ."

But, like our expressions of demarcation, they had devised a system of swearing by all sorts of things, carefully avoiding the name of God. Underneath this system was the dangerous dichotomy which Jesus exposed. What concerned him really was that God was considered a partner only of those agreements in which his name was used. All others were taken to be devoid of the binding and judgment of his presence. This was a fragmentation of life which denied that God is the Lord of all life. He is a part of the insignificant as well as the more clearly spiritual matters of life. No one can exclude God from any transaction. Everything we say and do has a relationship to him.

This brings into focus the careless use of words in our time. No wonder we find it difficult to communicate our faith! We often say more, or less, than we mean in order to create an impression or get a desired result. We hold some things as sacred and others to be used as it best suits our particular plans and convenience. Because we are like those ancient Jews, we think God can be excluded from aspects of life we would rather not expose to his judgment. But he hears—be sure of that.

We use words for prevarication, equivocation, evasion, and verboseness. Prevarication is the attempt to deceive by using words which in some sense are true, but which are intended to mislead the person who hears them. The half-truths, shaded truths, adjusted truths of all of us fall into this category. We say one thing to convey a thought which can be taken two ways.

Equivocation is the use of words which have several meanings. The equivocator intends to use one meaning in words while another is actually true. This happens when we say one thing and mean another. When our words are pressed for meaning, we are above reproach, but our intent is less than honest. Closely coupled with this is the use of words to evade truth. We use words to keep away from some subject. Talkative people are often evasive by using words to keep the conversation away from some subject which is painful or difficult.

But fulsome verbosity is a most common use of speech to distort. This device is the use of words to say more than we really mean. Into this category fall the solicitous use of compliments to manipulate, overstatements to create an atmosphere, and powerful terms of friendship or relationship which are not yet a reality. This misuse of profound, emotion-packed words without commitment of mind and energy to responsible expression of the life the words imply is very common in our everyday speech. Words bring a response of trust, infuse a sense of confidence, beget love and assurance, and foster closeness between people. But they are a rape of personality if they are not truly meant.

Whenever we talk too easily without responsibility, gossip, criticism, and sarcasm flow thoughtlessly from our lips. We can depreciate character, raise suspicion, and destroy another person's career by careless words. From our mouths can come blessing or curse. Talk is cheap, but its results can be very costly. This is the reason Jesus looked on words as sacred: "I tell you," he said, "on the day of judgment men will render account for every careless word they utter." (Matthew 12:36.) Many of us have lost our right to be heard concerning our faith because of the careless words we have spoken about others. People will not share with us or listen to us because they fear that what we have said about others we may say about them. The lines of communication have been cut by our use of words as a source of false security through depreciation of someone else. The Christian communicator who learns the sacredness of words uses them with utmost care.

But words are also sacramental. They are an outward sign of an inner condition. What we say, or refuse to say, is an undeniable projection of what's inside. Jesus was disturbed by the necessity of oaths to prove a man's honesty because this was a blatant admission of an evil world in which words were no longer a true expression of what was inside a man. Trust and confidence have broken down when a man's life is not adequate to confirm his words.

Jesus forced his listeners to see that words are divided from inner character. Elsewhere He said, "Either make the tree good, and its fruit good; or make the tree bad, and its fruit bad; for the tree is known by its fruit. How can you speak good, when you are evil? For out of the abundance of the heart the mouth speaks." Jesus came to communicate the love and forgiveness of God which would enable a man to be absolutely honest and open with himself and others. The deep inner transformation would provide a healing which would bring forth the fruit of authentic, creative, loving words. A life under his management would be so free from ambivalence that a man would not have to use words to cover or confuse.

But this leaves us with some personal questions! Are our words an authentic expression of what we think and feel? Is what we say stronger than an oath could ever be? Are we free to let people know us as we are?

Finally, I believe Jesus meant words to be solidifying. He said that our communication should be simply "Yes" and "No"; that anything more than that would come from evil. What he meant was that there is to be a simple directness among people who trust one another. The need for defensive explanation, self-justifying discourses, and tedious criticism is gone. The Christian family, the church, and Christian friendship are to be marked by such a deep trust of each other that what a person says is accepted without question. There is no need to juggle words, try to say the "right" thing, or create an atmosphere. Jesus Christ has liberated us from that!

Paul said, "For in Christ there is a new creation; the old has passed away; behold, the new has come." The new creation for

Paul was the power of Christ, releasing the inner man from all sorts of tension, fear, ambiguity, and duality. He was now free to be absolutely himself—the new self Christ had created within him. This was the basis of true fellowship with others. "Therefore, putting away falsehood, let every one speak the truth with his neighbor." Then Paul gives the deeper secret. "For we are members one of another." The reason for this is that we are inseparable parts of the body of Christ. We cannot distort the truth with one another without doing harm to ourselves and the whole body. Mutual trust, complete confidence, and unreserved openness were, and are, to be the identifying marks of a living church.

John wrote to the early church that as we walk in the light of Christ we can have honest fellowship with one another. This means that we can speak what we have to say to each other frankly in Christ's light. We need not conceal our insights to be spoken behind one another's back. In his light, all is exposed for mutual help and healing. Words which express the love of Christ to each other need not be guarded, for we belong to each other.

The church is the laboratory of life in which we learn how to use words to communicate love. The world becomes the place where we express what we have learned.

Words are one of God's great gifts for the ministry of the laity. Used under his guidance and filled with his power they can communicate his love, explain his truth, express his assurance, and impart his hope. They can challenge and comfort, uplift and encourage. I am always delighted when I am able to deploy a vital "member-minister" from our church in some situation of need. There is a growing number of people on whom I can depend to use the gift of words coupled with practical caring with someone I know needs help. These are people who are alive in their own faith, can communicate grace, and know how to talk about Christ and the Christian life simply and clearly. They know how to listen with patience and speak the truth with love.

I received a call from one of these communicators in the evening of the same day that I had received all these other requests for help. I was encouraged when the voice on the other end of the line said simply, "Just checking in for duty. I have a free evening and am ready for anything. Anyone you need me to see?"

I gave him one of the cases, and he followed through for weeks afterward. He earned the right to speak through persistent concern. Then he was able to talk about what Christ meant to him, what he had learned in similar problems, and how the people he was working with could find power for their lives.

Marshall McLuhan is right: the medium is the message. Our words cannot be separated from what we are. This man's life and concern for others made his words ring with reality.

🌲 the power of life as it was meant to be

12 / the power of a twentieth-century piety

Jesus' teaching on piety could be entitled "Religious Games Pharisees Play—Then and Now." The three acts of the comedy could be "Alms for the Love of Self," "Praying to People," and "Mighty Masks." As we watch the drama unfold, we laugh heartily. But then we are sobered, for we realize that our own lives have been portrayed before our eyes. We are stunned—we have been laughing at ourselves!

The Pharisees had taken almsgiving, prayer, and fasting and used them for self-aggrandizement. This alarmed Jesus because he was deeply concerned about how a man outwardly expressed his relationship with God. He was critical of any practice which was used to gain status and recognition from others and eventually became a substitute for humble dependence on the power of God's Spirit alone. He exposed piety which had become "piosity"—an end in itself and not a means of power to be used in ministry to others. His sharp wit pricked the bubbles of self-conscious pride and pretentiousness. He tried to help the Pharisees laugh at themselves so they might find life.

Once we have experienced God's grace and trusted him with the control of our lives, the new level of life must be nurtured by a creative discipline which enables us continually to open our minds to him and discover the fresh guidance and power he is ready to give. We cannot live on stale grace. Like the Israelites, we must gather the manna of life anew every day. Piety of any kind is under fierce attack in our day. But after the critics have had their day in court, we are still faced with the necessity of finding an authentic, ordered life under Christ's lordship. The insights he gave the Pharisees on how to practice their piety provide us with direction for our life today.

First of all, Jesus teaches us how to give of ourselves. He incarnated a love which was beyond reciprocal giving with a demand of return. His life and death exposed the self-giving essence of "in spite of" love. This love neither bartered for a desired result nor depended on the adequacy of the recipient. It was free and unencumbered by the baggage of judgment. This is the kind of love we have received and are called to give. It is the only creative reason for almsgiving.

Almsgiving was one of the most sacred tasks of the pious Jew. Because it was not required by religious law, it gave the donor extra merit. But it became so important that the same word is used for almsgiving and righteousness. The word "alms" means good works or acts of charity. What Jesus said will have meaning to us if we think of his challenge as pertaining to any aspect of our giving of what we are or have.

Jesus used a humorous metaphorical image to expose the wrong kind of giving: "When you give alms, sound no trumpet before you." We can imagine the side-slapping laughter that produced! A trumpet was used to call people to worship or to announce the times of prayer. His listeners could picture a man on the way to the Temple to give alms with a trumpeter marching before the ostentatious giver to announce to everyone that he was on his way to be generous. How absurd! Yet, how true of many of us. The only difference is that when the trumpeter does not play our tune loudly enough, we blow our own horns. But our volume and tempo are often subtle. We have learned how to draw attention to ourselves, our good deeds, and our accomplishments in ways that sound very magnanimous.

The classical meaning of the word *hypocrite* is "actor in a play." The hypocritical Pharisees were acting out their religious dramatics for the wrong audience. Though the box office returns were high, God was not in the audience. Their carefully staged religiosity had good returns in the admiration of others. Jesus wanted them to know that they would have a receipt marked "paid in full" from the people, but not from God.

This kind of ostentation gives illegitimate birth to the wrong kind of piety. It is not satisfied with the assurance of God's love; it must have the accolades of people. This is what disturbed Jesus. He saw how desperately the Pharisees needed people's approval. He seemed to be suggesting a freedom from people. He wanted us to love people so much that we would no longer need them. As long as we are dependent on people's response, we will calculate the giving of ourselves to them in chameleon-like adjustment to create the right impression.

What will people think? This is a familiar, oft thought, if not spoken, question. We all need and want the approval of the others who are significant in our lives. But some of us become so conscious of the opinions of others that we must have their confirmation to be secure. The danger of this is that we shape our lives around their ideas so much that we lose our individuality. Courage is replaced by conformity and decisiveness is diluted by the need for acceptance.

We can make gods out of the forceful people in our lives. We can practice or reject what we believe to be admired and assured by them. We are constantly onstage, playing out our piety or negating it, depending on the audience. The result of this is that our faith is the ineffective reproduction of someone else and we do not become the unique, free persons God calls us to be.

Not only do we use our piety to get approval, we use it as a manipulative device to get a desired response. We need people to fulfill our image of them. We cannot release them to be themselves because what we have made them fulfills something which is weak or lacking in us. Individuality is negated, personal freedom is sacrificed, and rebellion in varied forms results. This happens when we parade our piety to create guilt or insecurity in another person. When we demand the response, this kind of distorted piety results in a judgmental attitude and puts people on edge to measure up to our standards.

I talked to a woman at a conference the other day. She told me the sad tale of her husband, who did not share her faith and convictions. Everything was wrong. After she had related his shortcomings in great detail, I asked her why she had married him and why she now expected him to be something he had never pretended to be. Her image of him was of an unspiritual man who probably would never experience what she had found. Her negative attitude and lack of joyous, winsome love was keeping him locked in the closet of her preconceptions. She had made him the problem of her life. The problem, however, was within her. She could not see her husband in his need for her love because of the confusion within her.

A young man under pressure from a religious friend said, "I get the feeling that I am never going to measure up until I say I believe the same things he does. He's more concerned about my conversion than he is about me."

The second set of "Religious Games Pharisees Play" deals with

104

the games they played with God. Jesus was profoundly disturbed at the misuse of prayer. For him, prayer was the very center of fellowship with God. In it a man opens his total self to God. It is conscious communion with God in which he speaks to us through the thoughts engendered in our minds, the guidance of the decisions of our wills, and the inspiration of our emotions.

We can see why Jesus was so critical of hypocrisy in attention-getting public prayers. Some background will help. Three times a day, 9:00 A.M., 12:00 noon, and 3:00 P.M., a good Jew would stop his work and turn toward Jerusalem and pray. The professionally pious arranged it so that at the time of prayer they could be seen by others. Prayer became a formal duty and not a dynamic dialogue. In his book *Prayer and Personal Religion* John B. Coburn says: "God is a Person. He is infinitely more than this, but He is at least this. And this is the place to begin, for if you think of God primarily as a Person, then when you speak to Him you can say, 'You' and 'I'. When He addresses you, He in turn speaks to a person and also says, 'You.' Thus a two-way personal conversation, set in personal relationship, can be set up. This personal conversation is the essence of prayer."

For Jesus prayer was not to change God's mind but to receive it. Prayer is not some idea we dream up of what is best or desired; it is a response to God who has placed the desire within us to pray. It begins with God, is motivated by God in the believer, and is returned to God in honest intercession and supplication. What a difference this makes in our praying! It is no longer an effort to get God's attention, but attentive listening to what he has to say about how we are to pray about some need which has been placed on our minds. Once we understand what he is ready to give, then we can pray with holy boldness. If this is true, then it is not so much that God answers prayer as it is that his answer or direction is already awaiting our prayer. It is in dialogue with him that he communicates not only the answer but what we are to be and do as a part of that answer. Prayer is reporting in for duty.

God wants most to bind us to himself and to one another. Therefore there are resources of his power which are released only when we pray. What he longs to give us and others through us is to be found in prayer. As we pray for others, God repatterns our minds about them and what they can be. We get a new picture of others from God's point of view. Therefore new love and acceptance grow in our attitudes toward them.

A friend of mine has a new working postulate, a scientific assumption, which developed as a result of this idea of prayer. "Act as if Jesus Christ were present *in* other personalities for his redemptive purpose, not my own very human precepts and predictions of where their weakness will take them." This man's long dealings with people in his ministry as a trial lawyer has sharpened his human skill at diagnosing people. He often sees them at their worst and most unattractive point. In the past he had formed judgments, and people reacted within the confines of those judgments. He allowed negative reactions to block the divine inflow. Then he began reading the Gospel of Mark to study how Jesus dealt with people. He tried to see what Jesus might have seen in the harlots, the lepers, the publicans, the blind, *before* these people were healed. My friend realized that he himself would have seen so many horrible, negative facts and prognoses that healing would have been impossible through him. The fact that Jesus got rid of the negative thinkers around Jairus' daughter before he could heal her impressed him. He realized the power of his negative pictures of people which frustrated them in becoming what God desired.

Then, in a dream, this man had a conversation with Christ. He awakened, and as the conversation continued, Christ seemed to be saying, "See through me, through my mind filter; through the source of joy, source of mirth, source of energy, source of health, of relaxation. I came to save that which is lost. Your mind has been lost in the pigsty and has fed on swine diet. You can love in positive image."

In that time of deep prayer, this man learned that ministering to people meant trying to see things through Christ's eyes, to ask for his vision on things, circumstances, people. He was refocused in a positive image. People who came to him for help were seen in the light of Jesus' potential in them, not as categories of weakness. He experienced the Christ filter for his mind.

Prayer is not for play acting. It is not for public recognition. When we do have an opportunity to pray with or for others in public, we are to pray to God, not to them. We do not need King James pronouns or rhetoric. Simplicity, directness, honesty, willingness, and openness to receive what God has prepared to give before we ask will have a ring of truth. It is a moving experience to hear another person talk frankly with God about our needs or some mutual challenge. But few things are as disconcerting as to hear a person give us directive advice in the guise of prayer to God. Perhaps this is the reason we are "put off" by pious people who try to straighten us out by telling God what we need while we listen. A clergyman in Cleveland was "complimented" on his prayers: "He prayed more eloquently to Cleveland than any other clergyman in the city!"

The third kind of game the Pharisees played was with the practice of fasting. Jesus knew the value of fasting to express self-denial and to become more sensitive spiritually. During the period of denial of usual oral satisfactions, a person could grow, listen more intently to God, and discover his direction for his life. But the purpose of expressing love to God had been lost in hypocritical role playing. The fasting was done for recognition and not for spiritual discipline.

Jesus was critical of the facial contortions the Pharisees went through to be sure others knew they were fasting. Some even used a white cosmetic to look more emaciated. They wanted to leave little doubt of their religious sacrifice. What was meant to be an inner source of spiritual growth became an outer mask of piety.

Some time ago there was a very moving pantomime on television which portrayed the problem of the masks of piety. Marcel Marceau, the French mime, portrayed a man who had a mask for every situation. He enacted, in a very vivid way, how the man changed his masks. The act reached its climax when the man could not get one of his masks off in time to adjust to a new circumstance. He yanked and pulled to no avail. He was caught without the right mask!

This is what happens to us when we try to look more spiritual than we are. We store up a bag of masks of how we envision a Christian "ought" to look and act and try to get the right mask on for each situation. The tragedy of this is that we seldom are ourselves, genuinely engrossed in the situation at hand. We play at being Christians. God's grace liberates us to dare to be unreservedly ourselves and express our true feelings. The kind of life which will attract the "happy" pagan is not some superior, "I've got all the answers because I know Jesus!" look, but a joyous celebration of life which radiates on our faces. When Moses came down from the mountain, "He did not know that the skin of his face shone." He was not concerned about how his countenance looked but about God and what he had given.

Whenever we worry about how our piety looks, we have probably stopped looking to God and his amazing love.

What is the kind of person with whom we can take off the masks? Think of the people who allow us to be ourselves. How do they communicate that permissiveness? What do we feel in their presence? What did they say or do to assure us that no new mask was needed? Are we that kind of person to others?

I knew a man whose face looked like a plastic surgeon had frozen it into a jolly smile. People were put off because they sensed that he was faking. Early in his Christian experience he was told that it was his obligation to be exuberant regardless of how he felt. He had lived with this cruel obligation until it had become a habit. But underneath that mask was an aching heart. He never allowed people to know him as he was. His dishonesty kept him unhealed in his inner self. One day his pastor was frank with him about some needs in his own life. He was aghast that a clergyman ever had frustration! But the honesty eventually freed him to be honest. He related how sick he was of pretending. After many long talks, he dared to be himself. He had faced many of the things which have kept him tense and is on the way to freedom. He may not be as "jolly" all the time, but he is radiant because of the healing which Christ is performing at the core of his personality.

The kind of piety Christ wills for us is immediate and genuine, focused in the needs of others; and it is free to laugh at mistakes, accept forgiveness, and begin again. We are not to study, pray, worship, and witness in order to gain God's approval, but we will do those things naturally.

Piety is for power. Whatever puts us in a position to receive God's power is creative piety. The new breed of humanity we have been talking about, who have come alive in their faith, have found certain things essential to stay alive. A quiet period each day is necessary to receive the reorientation of their lives around God's marching orders for that day and its concerns. The Bible and the daily newspaper, fortified by current and classical devotional guides, provide the spiritual and intellectual stimulus for growth as persons. They keep a careful list of the people and needs God has placed on their hearts and ask, "Lord, what do you want me to say or do today to incarnate your answer to these situations?"

Deep fellowship with others is also an essential ingredient of the new life. Many are in small groups where they can see themselves honestly and gain power to change. Most pray for and seize opportunities to witness to others about what they have found. They are part of a worshiping congregation and are faithful in participation in the renewal of the church.

But these things which have been a part of pietism since the seventeenth century are not ends in themselves for either earning a right relationship with God or impressing others. Piety is like eating. We must be nourished to stay alive and live healthy lives. But just as eating can be overemphasized in either gluttony or culinary artistry, so piety too can lose its purpose to nurture. It must always be a part of "equipping the saints" for ministry. The task of caring for others, changing society, and healing suffering is so great that we dare not minister on our own strength. There is no need for the swing of the pendulum between social action and piety. They are both part of the style of life Jesus offers. One without the other is heresy.

13 / breakthrough to power

Jesus' cure for anxiety is anxiety. Is this a clever play on words? I think not. He suggests a creative anxiety which alone can burn out the smoldering fires of neurotic anxiety. His dynamic sweep of truth moves from the false causes of anxiety to the introduction of the reason for creative anxiety, and then to the practical word on where to begin. "Do not be anxious about your life . . . Seek first the kingdom of God . . . Take no thought for tomorrow . . ." are three steps of a breakthrough to power for daily living.

First, Jesus deals directly with false, surface anxiety. He brings to mind the categories which set our thoughts darting off to our own personal needs. What we eat, drink, wear—ah, these are the cares of life! Earning a living, paying our bills, keeping in style, maintaining our image, providing the comforts and necessities of life harass us all. But then Jesus shows the absurdity of anxious worry.

By the use of clever comparison he helped his listeners remember the providence of God. He reminded them of the birds of the air which depend on the providence of God and the flowers which live in beauty for but a day and are used to feed the oven fires. The whole point is that if God cares for birds which live for a brief time and the anemone which lives a few hours, will he not care for his children who are to live forever? If God lavishes infinite pains on these things, brief though their span of life is, how much more will he care for his human children who are to live eternally. How absurd anxiety is in this light! It cannot change our stature or our situations. A note of humor is parenthesized. A cubit, eighteen inches, cannot be added to a man's height, however much he worries. Nor can his fretting change the "unchangeables" in life. These surface anxieties summarize the care over the necessities of life which demand so much time and energy. "Well—that's life!" we say.

And that's what makes Sammy run! But it's not what really makes Sammy anxious. It's only what sets off our anxiety syndrome. The problems of life stir up our deeper needs, inadequacies, and tensions. And it is at this deeper level that Jesus seeks to heal us. He seems to be saying, "Don't get entangled with worry over the necessities of life and miss the purpose of life." As Helmut Thielicke put it, "False care is not combatted with an artificial and forced carefreeness—this would be sterile make-believe and would lead to nothing but an ostrich policy. Care can only be cured by care. Care about many things can be cured only by care about 'the one thing needful.'"

That prepares us for Jesus' second phase of a breakthrough to power. The one thing needful is to seek first the kingdom of God and his righteousness. This is the creative anxiety. To seek the kingdom and righteousness presents us with the ultimate question of life. To "seek first" is to urgently ask for and live as searching for God's will; to question our purpose, our reason for being, and our destiny. This anxiety is creative in that it prompts us to deal with issues of eternity. Could it be that we have lived our lives in anxious fretting about the trivia of life and missed

112

God's will for us in crucial relationships? There's really something about which to be anxious!

Paul Tillich has worked out the nature of this deeper kind of anxiety.[1] He distinguishes several types. He speaks of the fear of nonexistence. We all fear dying; but more than that, we fear living without the dynamic of faith which will assure us of living forever. We are anxious about eventually fading into nothingness. Have we come into a relationship with God now which death cannot end, by accepting his love by faith? A second type of depth anxiety is that of emptiness and meaninglessness. At the nerve center of life we all must find a meaning which gives purpose and direction to the multiplicity of our involvements. When we do not have this, we have a feeling of uselessness. We all need significance to our lives and will always experience anxiety until life is anchored in something which we know to be essential in God's strategy. Few things are more exasperating than the dull anxiety of boredom and insignificance.

Another aspect of this deeper kind of anxiety is guilt and self-condemnation for little goals and easy satisfactions. When we finally ask, "What have I done with the gift of life?" then we are vulnerable to true anxiety. When the waste of time, gifts, relationships, opportunities, drives us into introspection about the drift of our lives, then we are ready to face our responsibilities in the fulfillment of our potentialities. Sin is not just little failures; it is separation from God and the dynamic life he intended for all of us. I believe that when we grapple with the tension which this creative anxiety causes, then we are on the way to the healing of our little, troublesome, daily anxieties. In the light of these greater

[1] *Systematic Theology,* I (Chicago: University of Chicago Press, 1951), 191-201, 252-89.

issues we can laugh with Jesus at our fretting over our inconsequential problems of living when life is at stake.

Exactly! Anxiety is to be the source of renewed fellowship with God. Therefore, we do not need to condemn ourselves or feel that we have denied our faith if we are anxious, but seek to discover what it is that is causing it and bring that to God for forgiveness or healing or guidance. Honor the uneasiness of anxiety within and respond to God more deeply than before. Be as honest as you can about the inner causes of anxiety. Get to the roots and receive God's healing love there.

This has happened to a woman with whom I have had prolonged counseling conversations. She was filled with distressing memories which robbed her of peace. Finally we listed these memories on a piece of paper. Then we considered each one in the light of God's forgiveness. Only when she forgave what others had done to her (or she had done to herself) and asked for God's healing of each memory specifically was she able to be free of the anxiety which had been so evident in her life.

Creative anxiety produces an awe and reverence within us. We dare not take God for granted; he is not our celestial busboy! We have no "rights" before him. We have disturbed his children and constantly corrupted his creation with our selfishness and pride. It is by his grace alone that we dare to say, "Our Father, we love you because you first loved us." Each time we feel satisfied with false security, he allows us to go through a period of spiritual dryness and need so that our confidence will not be in our own spiritual achievement but in him alone. He is more concerned about our character than our comfort.

In this way we can accept the positive potential of our surface anxieties in life. Like hunger, anxiety alerts us to the fact that there is a need to be met within us. God will not let us go. He will disturb and alarm us about the blocks within us, areas in which we need to grow, relationships which need healing, and projects which need his guidance. Anxiety can be the prelude to new spiritual power.

A good example of this is in the life of Archbishop William Temple. He tells of an anxious, agonizing night when he had a difficult choice to make. "I tried to concentrate all my desires on knowing clearly what was God's will for me. I do not know how the hours went." He struggled with the decision until the answer was clear. The anxiety drove him back into deeper fellowship with God because he knew that the decision he must make was too great and the potential mistakes too costly for him to do it alone. That's the creative anxiety of seeking first the kingdom of God—his will and rule.

How about you and me? What have our anxieties driven us to—despair or discovery, frustration or fellowship?

This truth about anxiety is the only answer for life in the "now." That leads us to Jesus' third step to freedom. If we seek first God's kingdom, then we will not only be free from care about the needs of today, but will be free of worry about tomorrow. What a joy it is to begin to live in each day as if it were our last. The biggest worries we have are those which never materialize. Sir William Osler was right: "If the load of tomorrow be added to that of yesterday and carried today, it will make the strongest falter." This is the reason he advised people to "undress" their souls at night and leave the cares of that day behind. Anticipation is the magnifying glass of the emotions. Balzac said, "After all, our worst misfortunes never happen and most miseries lie in anticipation." But only those who have been driven back to God through deeper anxiety can be free to live in each day to the hilt. When the ultimate anxiety has been met, then tomorrow has less power of fear. We can bear the unbearable, do the undoable, pass the breaking point and not break.

Carlyle built a soundproof chamber in his house in Chelsea. All sound was excluded for silence to write—except the crow of a cock owned by a neighbor, once at night and once in early morning. Carlyle complained and the neighbor said that the cock crowed only so seldom. "But," Carlyle said to him, "if you only knew what I suffer waiting for that cock to crow!" There are a lot of us like that in life, harassed and suffering because we are waiting for something disastrous to happen. Creative anxiety about ultimate things alone can cure that!

When we are liberated from tomorrow and its potential needs and fears, we are able to invest ourselves completely in today. Suddenly people and situations become vital, important, and interesting because they have our "now" concern perhaps for the first time. Don't wait to live. All we have is now—the future will be shaped by what we do with this moment. Thank God for the anxiety felt today which signals our ultimate need, so when that has been met we can get on with life as it was meant to be. This is what Miguel de Unamuno, the Spanish mystic, wished for his friends: "And may God deny you peace, but give you glory!"

14 / the liberating power of affirmation

"I was a slumbering Christian. I learned the faith at my mother's knee and never left the church, even when I was wrestling with God over the nature of belief and the validity of the Christian claim. But I had never tasted the promises of God until I was chosen to be an elder on the session.[1] Here my commitment to Christ took on a new quality.

"The session was thinking through the hard question of where we were going as a church. I kept asking, 'What am I doing here?' and then I began to realize that I had been called to help contribute to unity. The session had to become a fellowship before we could find God's will and do it."

This was said by a leading church officer on our session during the birth and growth of the renewal program of our church. It was during this period that we discovered the liberating power of affirmation and learned how to communicate it in small groups. What happened to the session became the model for groups which developed later.

I had learned through previous experience and observation that

[1] The session is the ruling body made up of elders and pastor in a Presbyterian church. It corresponds to an official board, vestry, or consistory in other denominations.

117

authentic, lasting renewal must take place through the leadership of the church. Too often it springs up in a corner of the church's life. It becomes esoteric and exclusive. The officers who are responsible for the church may become suspicious and defensive. In some cases dynamic renewal has split churches because it did not begin at the heart of the church's life in the boards and then pulsate out into the church's whole life. Often pastors are least open and free with the "significant others" on the responsible boards, who become a focus of their egos as leaders. Pastors are reluctant to be known where they feel they must succeed. This creates an unreal atmosphere and cripples free, authentic relationships. So, as a substitute, they often take the easy alternative of sharing their deepest spiritual adventure with those they find it easy to be with and who respond readily because they think and feel alike. It is a longer and more difficult way through the boards, but it is ultimately more creative for the renewal of the church as a whole. When this is done, the thorny questions of social action, which eventually follow any period of spiritual renewal, can be faced and answered by renewed people in positions of leadership who can face the issues and give direction to the church.

When I assumed my post as pastor in Bethlehem, I was determined to move ahead in a renewal program only as quickly and as far as our session was enabled by God to move. I committed myself to spend time with session elders so that deep relationships of mutual caring and love could be born. We lunched, golfed, went to parties, and spent long hours together to know one another. We visited each others' homes and became acquainted with the joys and sorrows of each family. As trust developed, many of the men were able to talk about their personal spiritual needs. Honesty became the basic ingredient of these

118

friendships. I tried to be myself and take off the masks of ministerial pretense. This helped them admit their false pride or defensive guilt about not measuring up to the awesome office of "elder of the kirk." They were freed from the necessity to be more spiritual than they were. There was time for fun, laughter at ourselves, and release from images. In it all, we were learning to affirm each other as human beings. What happened later was a natural result.

My dream was that the session would live together in such a way that the congregation would begin to sense what Christian relationships were meant to be and be able to say, "That's what the whole church is meant to be!" As I look back, I realize that this is just what happened. We became in experience what we wanted the church to be as a whole—we became the church to enable the church. What we envisioned should happen to the church happened first with us.

We wrestled with the question: "How can a church help people to know and care for each other and participate in something crucial together?" We realized that the true sense of the church is difficult to experience in larger, impersonal meetings and formal, ordered worship.

Matthew 7:1-14 became our charter for renewal. Here Jesus deals with how his style of life is to be lived out with others. Each aspect delineates what affirmation means. "Whatever you wish that men would do to you, do so to them . . ." is the golden rule of affirmation in life together. For Jesus, this meant three crucial things which we tried to discover and practice together.

First it means that we are to be free of condemnatory judgment. Nothing stifles a ministry of affirmation as much as negative judgments about people who do not meet our standards, preconceptions, and requirements of adequacy. It makes the church a "house of judgment," as Thielicke calls it, and sets multiplied rejection in motion. We faced the danger of this and tried to learn the meaning of Jesus' challenge, "Judge not, that you be not judged." We learned there was a great difference between God-given intellectual wisdom and spiritual discernment and censorious blame of human inadequacy and sharp-tongued depreciation. Our judgments will be judged by God! We are to express the same mercy we have received from God in our failures. The more we experience the judgment of God on our lives and receive the grace he offers in forgiveness, the more we will be able to share our insights about another graciously. We are to affirm a person in his efforts to be honest with himself, share his struggles to be free from debilitating personality problems, empathize with his failures, and strengthen his efforts to begin again.

In this context we tried to understand the second aspect of Jesus' clarification of how to share our lives with each other. His words, "Do not give dogs what is holy; and do not throw your pearls before swine, lest they trample them underfoot and turn to attack you," have been difficult for biblical expositors through the years, but we believe they give a key to answer very important questions which arise every time a group begins to go deep. How honest shall we be? How much can we allow people to know us as we are? When is it right to give an insight which may be more than others in the group can handle? Jesus' caution is about too much too soon under the wrong conditions.

We have thought of it this way: dogs and swine cannot appreciate or appropriate the holy or the valued pearls. Jesus uses humorous hyperbole again. People are not dogs or swine, of course, but the temper of the group may not be ready for what we have to say about ourselves or others and may react vigorously. After varied experiences of living and working together, caring practically for each other, and participating in mission together, the atmosphere became receptive to increasingly deeper sharing. We affirm another person by allowing him to say as much about his needs as he is ready to share. There should be no hidden agenda of "when" or "how" for people to achieve. For each of us the challenge is not to be dogs or swine who trample on a person's sharing of himself with either criticism or indiscretion outside the sacred bounds of the group.

A third aspect of affirmation is expressed in prayer. We affirm another when we listen to his concerns, help him clarify the thing he wants most to claim from God in prayer, and then actually pray with him in the group and for him several times each day between meetings. A phone call a few days after a meeting reminding a person that we are persisting in prayer for the thing he is facing or attempting communicates affirmation. Paul told the Romans, "Without ceasing I mention you always in my prayers." Relationships are galvanized by this kind of mutual concern.

But the kind of prayer Jesus discussed here is not easy or flippant. His Aramaic words were translated into the Greek present imperative which means that we should always go on doing something. The command could well be translated, "Go on asking, go on seeking, go on knocking." Note the progression of intensity in the words. *Ask* is a gentle word, *seek* is a word of intense involvement, and *knock* is a word of importunity and persistence. It takes little energy or even thought to ask. When we seek, we become partners with God in finding the creative answer to our prayers. Prayer is not just idle musing about alternative possibilities; it is an active search for the answer under God's guidance. But how much do we want our answer?

121

Enough to persist? To knock means we have sorted out the alternatives and really want what God wants for us.

"Keep on praying" seemed to be the word for our life. Often we were not ready for an answer. But when concerns were talked through and prayed about persistently, amazing results occurred in people's lives.

The same officer I quoted above went on to say how he saw this take shape. "At first some of our members were suspicious. We were on our guard against letting down our masks. Gradually our resistance was broken, and by the end of the first year we had learned that God wanted us elders to be the church in microcosm putting fellowship with Christ at the center of our business."

To accomplish this goal, the elders went on a series of overnight retreats. Here they analyzed their own relationship to Jesus Christ and together asked the question, "What does God really want of us as a church?" They came to see that the church needs to be four things in order to call, equip, and deploy the ministry of the laity. It is to be a worshiping congregation, a healing communion, a training center, and a commissioning station. To focus more specifically on their calling, they divided into six departments—worship, *koinonia* (the Greek word for fellowship), nurture, evangelism, outreach, and stewardship—to evaluate all that they were presently doing and to seek new directions.

In all of this I felt that my function has been not to project a program onto the church but to lead its elected officers into the kind of fellowship and concern where they would discover together the forms their life as a church should take in order to prepare people to participate in Christ's mission in the world. A conviction grew that institutions, like people, become what

122

they envision themselves to be. Therefore, a five-year plan was adopted which encompassed the deepest thinking and planning which came out of these times together. It is fascinating to realize how many of these goals have been reached by God's power. The picture of the church we held before us is what we became.

The retreats and definite periods for sharing, study, and prayer in each regular meeting drew us together in healing fellowship. It was only natural that we wanted to have the whole church experience what we were discovering. What we were finding was so much deeper than the word "fellowship" conveyed that we began to use the Greek word for fellowship, *koinonia*. This forced us back into the true interpretation of sharing and participation in Christ with each other that we find in the early church. We found that we were to be to each other what Christ had been to each of us. Several of the elders were put into what was called the *koinonia* department and charged with the responsibility of evolving ways of helping the church as a whole to participate in true *koinonia*.

The result of this was that we held retreats for the members like those we had been through together. The elders became the discussion leaders and witnessed to what they were discovering. For a time these were monthly in the calendar. Later they were replaced wth bimonthly renewal conferences, but the pattern of program remained the same. There were times for challenging exposition of the biblical meaning of the church and the Christian style of life; times for personal stories from people about their growing faith; times of sharing in depth in small groups; and quiet time for individual re-evaluation.

The second phase of the *koinonia* strategy was to call together about seventy people who were released and renewed in these retreats and conferences for a series of leadership training sessions. This training culminated in a presentation of the challenge of small group leadership. Specific instruction on the dynamics of group life was given. These people were designated as group enablers and their names were printed in the church bulletin on the Sunday morning when the opportunity of small groups was presented to the congregation. We called them *koinonia* groups. The purpose of each group was to be the church in miniature. We explained the threefold function of each group in the light of the biblical meaning of the church. They were for study and proclamation of the gospel; for fellowship in depth relationships of mutual caring and concern; and for the discovery and development of ministry by individual members and the group as a whole. The trained leaders were challenged to start groups and others in the congregation joined them as they were prompted and led by Christ. The result was that groups of varying sizes and composition grew throughout the congregation. There were couples' groups, mixed groups of varying ages, professional groups, housewives' groups, men's luncheon groups, and teen-age groups. We kept Christ's charter for affirming group life continually before us.

The next step in launching this program was the establishment of monthly training meetings led by one of the pastors along with several elders. A study guide for the groups was developed, and each month a representative of each group came for spiritual and intellectual preparation as discussion leaders for subsequent meetings of their groups in that month.

The content for study varied as the program grew. Biblical exposition, current books on personal faith and church renewal, and penetrating confrontations of social problems were used. Many of the groups used a devotional booklet called *Come Alive,*

published quarterly by the pastors, which provided a daily meditation in preparation for the sermon on the following Sunday.
Each day's guide contained a thought for the day, scripture, and
meditation which would be part of the sermon. These books
contained questions for small group discussion for each week.
The congregation focused in on one book of the Bible each year.
The Sunday sermons exposited the content, the groups discussed
the implications for daily life, and people tried to implement in
their ministry in the world what they found.

The most effective groups have three phases to almost every
meeting. There is no rigidity on the timing of these periods,
and often one flows naturally into the next with little formal
demarcation. But any dynamic meeting has time for study and
discussion; sharing of personal needs and an inventory of each
person's ministry and the group's united outreach in mission;
and time for spoken and silent prayer. When this simple discipline is followed with freedom, the group grows in vital
koinonia.

Some groups have failed, while others have had to be sub-
divided and new people added. We are free to take emerging
leadership from one group and begin others. People are released
from any need to have successful groups. When a group is ineffective, we admit it and help in the rearrangement of people
or in diagnosing and treating the difficulty.

Since everyone who joins our church must participate in an
inquirers' group for concentrated study of the faith and the
mission of the church, these groups of new members make
natural *koinonia* groups. A group enabler from the church mem-
bership is a part of each inquirer's group and is ready to take
those new members who are willing into a small group experience after the inquirers have joined the church. Many of those

who go through the inquirers' group experience find a liberating faith and a sense of ministry for the first time. The *koinonia* group becomes a crucial part of the conservation of the new life Christ has given.

In it all, the most important achievement of the *koinonia* program is that people have learned how to affirm themselves. We have found that self-affirmation overflows in affirmation of others. When we have been authenticated by Christ's love and feel a strategic purpose which makes life exciting, we are suddenly aware of a capacity of liberating love for others. We sense Christ's desire to incarnate his affirmation of others through our words, expressions, involvements, concern, listening, and loving. We are to be with other people in such a way that what we say, do, and are gives them a rebirth of significance. The extent to which we become great people is the extent to which we are graciously affirming. We are all needy people: we need reassurance and validation, and we need to be told that our life is recognized and appreciated. No one is exempt from this need! Verbal expression is absolutely necessary to penetrate the layers of self-distortion and negation. Then involvement with a person in his concerns validates the expression. Most of us are aware of the things in our lives which we need to change. When others believe in us and hold us to our best, we are able to change and grow.

There is no limit to the power a church can have which becomes a center of affirmation. It will move out into society as a mighty force with freedom and joy. And what we will do in society as a power structure is the "life or death" question of the last third of the twentieth century for the church.

15 / the church as a power structure

Before we had a symbolic cross in our chancel, visitors used to ask, "Where is the cross in this church?" Little did they know that they were asking a very important question—far more important than the whereabouts of a symbol. Recently another visitor asked an even more searching question. He had seen the chancel before we had the symbolic cross. Now, noting the new addition of the cross, he asked, "Tell me, now that you have a cross, do you find that the church is any more aware of its meaning for life?" What would you say about your church?

How we answer is crucial. It is now, in the last third of the twentieth century, that I believe it will be determined whether the institutional church will become a viable force in Christ's plan for the transformation of our society or whether it will be bypassed as an unusable instrument of change and renewal. The issue is that of the cross. If we will not use the power entrusted to us through the cross, Christ may have to use other people and groups to get his work done in these very revolutionary times. He has given us freedom to choose. This is the most crucial choice before the church today.

Life under the cross means relentless reformation. In each age,

Christ is actively reforming his people—exposing, breaking, frustrating any organization of his people which stifles renewal and any institutionalism which blocks vital incarnation. He does not rest in any period until his church is humble, authentic, self-denying, courageous, outspoken, and involved in human suffering and social injustice. He will not let his people enjoy him without encounter with the world he died to save. He persists until our religiosity chokes in our throats and our piosity putrefies in our bones. He is suffering new Golgothas in the world wherever people are in need. If we want to find him we must go where he said he would be. "If any one serves me, he must follow me; and where I am, there shall my servant be also." (John 12:26.) Is your church where he is?

As never before in Christian history, society's needs must write the agenda for the local congregation. Many of the tragic social issues which entangle our communities exist because individual Christians did not live out the gospel and because the congregation did not exercise its divinely ordained responsibility to be a power structure to bring pressure for change in injustice and evil. Laws and ordinances in opposition not only to our constitution but also to the implications of our faith have been tolerated, and customs have been perpetuated which disenfranchised and debilitated people because of economic or racial status. The local congregation must repent of the intolerable sin of having often coexisted with horrendous social wrongs all around it and in the relationships of its people. We have preached and prayed our way to power in American life while ghettos were collecting the rejected Americans. In many metropolitan centers, following the movement of people who could not tolerate the tensions of the changing neighborhoods, we have moved from troubled and congested urban areas. We have grown strong in safe suburbs

128

while God's gift of the inner city was rejected because of its uncertain or questionable wrappings. Leaders among the laity in many cities were often in positions of power in industry, community organizations, and political parties, but that power was too seldom used to correct the problems of these cities as they grew. The painful issues of Christian social action were overlooked or never crystallized as crises of conscience for churchmen.

There are few institutions more resistant to change, more hostile to the demanding implications of the cross, more anesthetized to the pain of human suffering than most institutional, local churches! They are slow to innovate; reaction to just criticism is violent; mobilization in an immediate need is difficult without conflict over the nature and extent of that involvement. Caution, fear of discord, peace at almost any price has become the tenor of congregational life. Outspoken, prophetic leaders are quietly domesticated or quickly discarded. An endless round of services, committee meetings, study groups, and church suppers give an illusion of purpose and direction while society aches for justice through the application of the very things which are preached, prayed, and discussed at often dull, boring church gatherings. The greatest tragedy, however, is that most congregations will not know—nor some even care—that Christ has moved on to others who may profess less but actually are more vitally involved in areas where he is at work.

The church is responsible—there is no escape. The America we have tolerated is the embarrassing aspect of America we have come to abhor. Much of what we have now is what we have allowed. Once again the plumb line of the cross is lowered. What we have built is out of plumb, and the foundation is made of sand. There can be no health in the institutional church until we confess our failures.

It is in this context that we must understand Jesus' conclusion to the Sermon on the Mount. In the parable of the two builders he declared the truth that we need to rediscover: there is an inseparable relationship between hearing and doing. We have done what Jesus feared we would do. He knew that we would have a fantastic capacity for diluting and emasculating the truth he spoke. He confronted the false prophets of irrelevant religion and warned against wolves in sheep's clothing. Ours are actually *sheep in wolves' clothing* who dissuade the flock from within. He anticipated us praying and singing our beautiful "Lord, Lord" without discerning God's will and doing it regardless of cost. Therefore, in a disturbing way he suggested that what he had said was not just the pleasant ramblings of another rabbi but absolutely essential truth about life which alone could be an adequate foundation for the storms which will come if we are obedient to him. He asserted his divine power and prerogative by saying that only he and his words could be a rock foundation. The wise builder was one who dug deeply and laid his foundation on the rock of hearing and doing what Jesus had said about life.

To hear and do! Ah, that's the rub! To hear and truly understand—that's hard enough. But to do—really to apply in costly action and involvement—that's something else again! And Jesus demands both. It's no easier to follow him now than it was then.

The narrow way of the cross looms before us. It is the cross of obedience. Live out the implications of life as it was meant to be and there will be a cross. It means death to our clever schemes, securities, and comforts, and it spells out the nature of our involvement wherever evil incarnate in human suffering must be confronted with the justice and love of God. It will not be easy. Every issue facing the church today has a slippery Caiaphas, a vacillating Pilate, a betraying Judas, and a centurion who will drive the nails because it's his job.

Hearing the good news of the cross and living out its implications in society is the only reliable rock on which to build the life of a congregation. When this happens, the church becomes a power structure. Our power is the cross! But we need to learn how to use this power entrusted to us.

In every local congregation there are those who are charged with developing the direction of that particular congregation. This group must wrestle long and hard over some very basic questions. "Where is Christ crucified anew in our community? What are the things which dehumanize and destroy people where they work, live, are educated, spend their leisure? What conditions of life contradict Christ's love for all men? If Christ walked the streets of our city, what would he expose, attack, and demand changed? What are these areas of suffering, unequal opportunity, injustice? How have the church and individual Christians perpetuated these evils? What are the specific things which would be done if we were completely under Christ's control and cared little for personal property, gain, reputation, or popularity? What are the long-range goals and the immediate steps to be taken?"

These are the questions our elders began to ask a few years ago. Our outreach department had many special meetings for prolonged study, discussion, and prayer. When they were ready, they brought their recommendations to the session. One of the retreats I mentioned in the previous chapter dealt exclusively with the implications of the cross for our specific ministry in the community. Because of the love and honesty which had been developed in this group through depth fellowship for months before, people spoke their minds and we struggled together to

131

know the mind of Christ. There was creative controversy. To speak of controversial issues is redundant. Any important issue is controversial. If there are no controversies gripping the officers of a church, then the church is dying, preserving the past, not praying for the best God has to give in the future. Deep, penetrating discussion on these controversies reveals whether we are living under the cross. It's never simple—Christ did not say it would be.

From these times together the "target areas" of particular need became clear. For example, one year we settled on five major focuses for our ministry in the community: housing for low-income people, particularly among minority groups, exchange of members with a black congregation, assistance to young black junior executives brought to the community by a local industry, involvement with the problems of Puerto Rican youth on the city's south side, and responsible care for the aged. The target areas were published for the congregation, preached from the pulpit as specific examples of how to become involved, adopted by organizations within the church as a guide for united action, and declared in the community. The church moved into action. Along with other congregations, we declared a holy war on these needs and the people and groups which were either causing them or condoning them. We learned about the untapped power the church can have to expose and exercise pressure for change.

Individuals within the congregation, who had often felt that the Sunday morning worship had been a call to arms but had not known who the enemy was or where to fight, now had insight and direction of how and where to minister. Our *koinonia* groups got into action when various groups adopted these targets for special concern. One of the discoveries we made was that exhortation is a vital gift of the Holy Spirit to group life. We are to spur one another on to the next step of obedience under the cross. This is done through careful analysis of community needs and ways Christ might use each of us in those areas. The group becomes the supportive fellowship for practical assistance and persistent prayer. We ask, "With whom has Christ called you to attack this problem? Find him and work out a strategy. Stand together and support each other."

People in positions of power began to see that they had been deployed by Christ in their jobs to press for change and new programs in industry and the community to solve these problems. We have learned again that in almost every social need there are a few people who can make a tremendous difference when the cross is their guide and they use their power to effect change.

One of these men said, "I'll expect you at work at 8:00 tomorrow morning. Your sermon made it sound so easy this morning. I want you to come and help me make some of the tough decisions I must make in the difficult, frustrating problems I must handle." There was a twinkle in the man's eye as he said this to me at a coffee hour after a service in which I had tried to touch on the implications of living out the gospel. He was jesting, of course, but a deeper truth registered. This man is on the firing line. He is responsible for drafting and carrying out his company's policies in areas of social justice. He has been entrusted with institutional authority and has gained respect through the years. Others listen to him and are willing to follow. His deepest concern is to rigorously apply his faith to his decisions. Often it is difficult to discover, discern, and do what God wants in a particular decision. He has to struggle in the gray areas and wrestle for the right answer. It's not easy to be a Christian!

Montaigne was asked to become mayor of Bordeau. He replied, with significant reservation, "I am willing to take the city's affairs on my hands, but not on my heart or liver." He felt his public service must not tax his health or strain his constitution. How very different is the reaction of a man I talked to recently who is working to integrate a union. "Often I am tempted to give up the struggle, but the love of Christ sends me back to my task again."

"Does it ever get at you?" I asked. His wife answered, "Sometimes he doesn't sleep very well. He really cares about what happens!"

That's the cross's driving power. The suffering Saviour is our disturbing example. Once we commit our life to Christ we begin a long and demanding experience of listening to what his gospel delineates for the common life and then daring to do it. We fail people in the church when we either oversimplify or underclarify the gospel for our time. The greatest tragedy, however, occurs when we do not help people sense that they are the church in the world and stand with them in times of costly obedience.

We know that we have hardly begun to discover what it means to be a power structure as a church. New issues arise; different target areas are given to us by Christ. There is often disappointment and temptation to become discouraged. But there is no turning back now—for us or any congregation. Our Lord asks us what he asked the disciples long ago: "Will you also go away?" And we answer with the disciples, "To whom shall we go? You have the words of eternal life."

Jesus was right: the foundation for the inevitable storms of life is built through application of his words. Admonitions become our character when we live in actuality the things he said. Message and Master together become our rock-like stability. Paul found this to be true. Christ was a sure rock for him. "For no other foundation can anyone lay than that which is laid, which is Jesus Christ."

16 / the authority of the authentic

I would be less than honest if I did not tell you that I believe it is impossible for us to live the Sermon on the Mount. If we have looked honestly at Jesus' demanding portrait of life, we all know that this is true. What he has outlined for us is so far beyond where we are, really, that we are tempted to throw up our arms in consternation and say, "Who could ever live that way in times like ours?" If we do not have this reaction, then we have not seen the quality of life Jesus has depicted for us. Anyone who reacts, "Well, that seems to be a good plan for life—let's get on with it!" or, "I have tried always to pattern my life according to the Sermon on the Mount!" has probably not come to grips with the profound challenge Jesus has put before us. The only authentic response is, "It's beyond me! I don't experience a joy like that, feel a love for others like that, care about the sickness of society like that, sense a power to live like that!"

That's just where Jesus wants us to be. The Sermon on the Mount is impossible! He meant it to be! The quality of life he has revealed can never be lived by human strength or redoubled effort. Those who have tried have ended up in false pride or

135

miserable failure. Jesus did not offer an easy guide for life to be lived for him; he revealed a level of life he would live in us. The Sermon on the Mount is a self-portrait. He is the life he taught. All that he said from the mount was in anticipation of when he would live this life in his people. When he said later, "These things which I have done, you shall do also—and greater things," he clarified the hope of a new life. By his power dwelling within us we are to do what Jesus did and live the life he lived.

Just before the ascension the answer was given to human impotency to live the life Jesus had lived and challenged men to live. "He charged them not to depart from Jerusalem, but to wait for the promise." What was the promise? "You shall receive power when the Holy Spirit has come upon you."

The Holy Spirit is Christ in the present tense. The eternal Spirit of God who had created, called, and sustained his people through the centuries, who had revealed his essential nature in Jesus Christ, would continue his ministry in the present enabling power within. B. H. Streeter put it plainly years ago in his book *The Spirit:* "What is the Holy Spirit? It is no other than the Spirit manifested in the life of Christ. If Christ is our portrait of the Father, He is no less our portrait of the Holy Spirit." More recently, Henry P. Van Dusen amplified that same truth: "The Holy Spirit affirms the intimacy of omnipotent Power discerned as to His character in Jesus Christ. The never-failing availability of that Power—His ready accessibility to each of us at every moment, of this the Holy Spirit testifies. But that intimate Presence is not some ghostly, mystifying specter; but the actual spirit of Jesus of Nazareth, now immediately present and yet the very Being of Ultimate Reality. The Holy Spirit declares God's omnipresence. Here, we think especially of God-near and

136

God-at-work in the souls of those ready and eager to receive Him." [1]

The Sermon on the Mount is Jesus' description of how he will live his life in us and through us. He promised that he would come and make his home in us. Paul learned this and exclaimed, "Christ in you, the hope of glory!" There is no hope of living life as it was meant to be without the power of the indwelling Christ. James Stewart puts it this way: "The life which flows from Christ into a man is something different, not only in degree, but also in kind. It is a new quality. There is a new creation, not just an intensification of powers already possessed, but the sudden emergence of an entirely new and original element wherever a man comes to be in Christ. He begins to live in the sphere of the post-resurrection life of Jesus." [2]

After Jesus finished the message from the mount, the people were astonished. He taught as one who had authority, not as the scribes. That means he taught with power which the religious scribes had never exemplified. Their rigid rules and formalism had never moved people. Jesus, however, won their attention and allegiance by an authentic authority validated by his own life.

That authority is now offered to us. The living Christ is our power to live a life which would be impossible with all of our self-effort and improvement programs. He will take our minds and think through them; he will heal our emotions and love through them; he will motivate our wills and guide through them; and he will live in our bodies and radiate through them. Life by the Spirit is the alternative to religion and trying harder.

"If I hear one more inspiring talk about the power of God and

---

[1] Henry P. Van Dusen, *Spirit, Son and Father* (New York: Charles Scribner's Sons, 1958), p. 176.

[2] James Stewart, *A Man in Christ* (New York: Harper & Row, 1935), p. 193.

the joys of the Christian life without someone telling me simply how I receive this power and get started in this new life, I swear I will stand up in the next meeting and scream!"

A fine religious churchman who did not know God said this to me recently at the end of a day of meetings at an excellent conference for men, sponsored by a major denomination. It had been a long, challenging day. We had heard great preaching and had participated in stimulating discussions. My new friend was stirred and disturbed. He had been told about the Holy Spirit and what life could be if he empowered a human life. But he had heard enough; he had spiritual and intellectual indigestion. "Tell me how!" was his plea. He needed someone to listen to his needs as a person and to tell him simply how to receive the Holy Spirit and how he could begin a life of fulfillment instead of frustration.

This man has vocalized the need many of us feel. Some time ago H. Wheeler Robinson clarified this same frustration: "The truths of evangelical Christianity remain true, but they seem to lack vitality. They seem to demand an active effort of faith for which the energy is lacking, like a great balloon with ample lifting power, if only one had the strength to grasp the rope."[3]

How would you have answered that man at the conference? Our temptation would be to give a quick and easy answer and offer him some spectacular emotional experience which would only intensify his frustration when his feelings faltered. He needed love and understanding and not more theory. He was laboring under the misapprehension that the Holy Spirit was some addendum to God. When it came down to putting what he believed into words, his idea of the Trinity was really three Gods

[3] H. Wheeler Robinson, *The Christian Experience of the Holy Spirit* (New York: Harper & Row, 1928), p. 4.

linked in some mystical way he could not articulate but which left him in a quandary. He was helped by learning that the Holy Spirit is not something separate from God, but is the Almighty God revealed by Jesus Christ and now present in the world. He was amazed to learn that his desire to "receive" the Holy Spirit was because the living God was already at work in his life creating the desire to know and experience the power which was at that moment impinging on his consciousness.

I shared with him an alliteration of four "R's" which had been helpful to me through the years: recognition, response, reception, and release. We talked for a long time about each step. (As we look back over the Sermon on the Mount, it is all there in Jesus' message.) We talked about how to recognize our need and the crises which crystallize that need. I listened intently as he talked about what these were in his life. My friend articulated the problem for most of us. "After all that we have said, I recognize my need all right and all that Christ can do, but there is something holding me back."

We had to go deeper. He was like most of us. We recognize our need but do not respond because we are blocked by unresolved memories of the past, unredeemed wishes for the future, and undedicated relationships in the present. Most of us are filled with conscious and unconscious reservations. We are dreadfully afraid of what might happen to us if Christ took complete control of our lives.

Wholeheartedness is the missing quality in contemporary Christianity. We are distracted by a multiplicity of commitments and fears. It is almost impossible for us to give ourselves to God because of the many frustrations that lurk within us. We are filled with doubts about ourselves which cause our uncertainty about the reality of Christ.

It is impossible to receive what God has offered until we have stopped striving and straining. As Søren Kierkegaard said, "You must give yourself to Christ unconditionally. Nothing, nothing, be it greatest triviality or something tremendously important in your eyes, must be put between yourself and Him that it becomes a condition. . . . No, the surrender must be unconditional." And I would add, it must be specific. We start where God has already begun. When we consider Christ's words, "Behold, I stand at the door and knock," is there any reason we cannot let him in? Be careful now—he is Lord and Master—anything in the way? Anything unresolved? We start there! Is all under his guidance and will? No? Then we can start there: marriage, children, work, future plans, money, resentments.

Next, my new friend and I talked about how to respond to the love which God had had for him through the years in spite of his neglect and subtle resistance. He found it difficult to acknowledge that this love was a gift which he could never deserve or earn, made to him as if he were the only person alive. When we got into the matter of receiving, we talked about a profound question the late David Roberts once asked: "What would happen if instead of hanging on to Christianity, or defending it, or taking it for granted, we could recognize that the reality of God is up to Him? What would happen if we realized that His forgiveness is not within our power and that we cannot guarantee it for anybody, including ourselves? Might not we then find that our relationship to Him—deep down in our lives—directly reflects what we are? Might we not discover the problem of sustaining faith each day is not one of hanging on, but of letting go—letting go of ourselves?"

He thought deeply about that. I shared with him my own and others' experiences of how life really began when we accepted

140

what had already been offered by God and turned the control of our lives over to his guidance and direction. To receive is to acknowledge him as Lord of all and accept his power for all the relationships and decisions of life.

When we got into release, the word *freedom* caught his imagination. His life was filled with the tension of self-effort. When I asked him what his life might be like if he were free, he began to picture for me areas of his life which were "up-tight," as he put it. Again I heard the familiar sense of irrelevancy so common in "good people." We talked about our world and tried to envision what Christ could do through him if he were willing. If he were changed, what would Christ change in his environment? He was quiet for a long time. The Holy Spirit he had asked about was obviously penetrating into his life. When I sensed he was ready, I simply said, "I believe the living Lord has been here with us all the time we have talked. Why don't we tell him how we feel about this whole matter?"

"That means prayer, doesn't it? What do I say? I want to mean it this time," he said. We discussed what his prayer of abandonment might be, and after a period of silence, this is what I remember he prayed:

"Living Lord, I am tired of trying to follow your example and be good on my own power. I haven't done very well, as you know! I have been religious in church, but I have never yielded the vital center of my own control of myself and my will to you. I believe that you are my Saviour, and now I want you to rule my life as Lord of everything—home, work, money, thoughts, goals, motivations—*everything*. You have promised that you would live in us. I know that this is why I was created, to receive and transmit your living Spirit. I yield myself without reservation. Come, Holy Spirit, take control—now and forever."

We have kept in touch by mail during the past year. There were many things to straighten out and a sick society where he lives in which to become involved. But he's on the way! What an impact on his church and company he has made! He speaks and lives with authority—the authority of an authentic life.

Wonderful things happen in very unexpected circumstances. The other evening I attended a human relations commission meeting. Before the meeting a Methodist layman, a black social worker, a Roman Catholic priest, and I were talking about the impotence of most Christians to face the needs of our time. The Methodist layman volunteered an experience which brought vitality to an otherwise perfunctory discussion. He related how he had come alive in his faith and had begun to realize the meaning of the things he had sung and prayed for so many years. How different church and society were now. The Roman Catholic priest looked at him intently, "My friend, you have received the Holy Spirit!"

The conversation deepened suddenly. Before we knew it, we were all sharing what had happened to each of us to lift us out of traditional, institutional religion to life. The touch of God's power had come to each of us in different ways. But we all had to admit that, until God had intervened and given us an assurance of his living power, we had trudged on doing our best with little joy.

But why does this happen so seldom? Is God playing favorites? No! He is persistently penetrating into each of our hearts. He is not hiding; we are! Most of us have to try everything else before we are able to pray, "I am out of power; I need the Holy Spirit; I am open to the Holy Spirit."

Calvin was right: "Man is spiritually dead until he is quick-

142

ened and wakened by the Holy Spirit." That is the great need in the church and in all of us today.

There is a benediction which has come to mean a great deal to many of us who are seeking to live an authentic life, empowered in every facet of our being by the indwelling Christ. "May the Living Christ go with you. May he go behind you to encourage you, beside you to befriend you in obedient ministry, above you to watch over you, within you to give you power, and before you to show the way."

The Lord goes before us! He precedes us! That's what we all need to know. As our cities smolder from race riots, as we nurse our grief over man's inhuman prejudice, as we wait with painful patience for the leaders to gather around a conference table to end hostilities in Vietnam, as we see human progress exposed as an inadequate basis for our lives, as we wonder where the next major world conflict will break out and demand our troops and resources, as we face personal loss of someone we have loved, and as we come to grips with the problems and challenges of our own lives, we desperately need to know that Jesus Christ, the hope of the world, is alive. He has conquered death! He goes before us to show us the way! There is no place where we can go where he has not been before us; there is no one with whom we must deal whom Christ has not prepared for us; there is no situation in which we are to live where he had not preceded us; there is no temptation, trial, or tragedy in which he has not entered before us; there is no joy or happiness we are to know which he has not prepared beforehand. The one who said, "I, if I be lifted up, will draw all men to myself" is the magnetic uplifting Lord who lifts us out of defeat and dejection and beckons us on to a life of hope.

We can endure anything with a hope like that. When our

hope is no longer based on human adequacy or ability or perfection, we can place our hope in Christ and face whatever life has to offer.

The Sermon on the Mount can be lived today as Christ lives it in us. Life as it was meant to be can be life as it actually is! We can live while we are alive for the rest of our lives. The world around us will be amazed and say, "They live as people with authority and power. How very different from the religious people they used to be!"

144